# Guide to Non-profits
# From the Trenches

*An Overview for Controllers, Treasurers, CPAs, and CFOs*

**Sheila G. Shanker CPA, MBA**
**www.webshanker.com**

First published by Sheila G. Shanker- CreateSpace  Oct. 2009

ISBN: 1448697662
EAN-13: 9781448697663.

Printed in the United States of America

This book is dedicated to my parents,
Myra Creimer Golgher and Marx Golgher

# TABLE OF CONTENTS

# CHAPTER 1

## *INTRODUCTION*

This book is the type of publication I wish I had had when I started my career working with non-profit organizations. It provides an overview of major non-profit areas for the finance professional. This is not a publication about basic accounting principles or concepts. It is not about opening your own non-profit organization.

While writing an online course about non-profits, I noted the lack of good, simple, general information about the non-profit world. So, this book was born to fill that void.

You could be a new Controller, Manager, Board member, or CFO working in the non-profit sector for the first time. You may have questions about operations or specific accounting issues, such as what the heck are "funds" or "net assets"?

This book is not solely about presenting you with dry information. It is about my personal experiences as well. Combining theory and personal experience, each chapter gives you information about an important facet of the non-profit world. The point is to make this book an overall resource of information.

Who am I to write this book? I am a finance/accounting professional with twenty years of experience in the non-profit sector. As a CPA and MBA with a background in auditing, management, and consulting, I have developed online CPE courses for professionals. My experience includes serving as the top finance person in many organizations, including Board of Directors.

Please note that, like everything in life, things change. The information provided in this book may change, and most likely, will change. As I write this, I hear talk of the IRS changing the "new" 990.

I hope you find this book informative and a basis for further research in the non-profit sector.

# CHAPTER 2

## *FUNDAMENTALS OF NON-PROFITS*

*"Wikipedia is a non-profit. It was either the dumbest thing I ever did or the smartest thing I ever did. Communities can build amazing things, but you have to be part of that community and you can't abuse them. You have to be very respectful of what their needs are."*

Jimmy Wales (Keynote Speech, SXSW 2006-founder of Wikipedia)

Wikipedia is one of millions of non-profits based in the U.S. providing goods/services to many communities. The non-profit sector is not a new fad. The U.S. has a long history of philanthropy. One of the first organized campaigns for donations was the "United Thank Offering," created by the Episcopal Church in 1889. Christmas Seals was founded in the early 1900s due to the spread of tuberculosis and other lung diseases. Other known charities, such as the Boy Scouts, National Association for the Advancement of Colored People and Goodwill were created between 1909 and 1913. The Rockefeller Foundation was established in 1913.

The largest non-profit organization is the Bill and Melinda Gates Foundation, with an endowment of about $30.2 billion, making it the biggest in the world. This foundation has committed billion of dollars in grants since its inception. (http:/www.gatesfoundation.org)

The non-profit sector is obviously a growing sector in the U.S. economy. In 1996, there were 535,930 non-profits registered with the IRS. In 2006, the number of non-profits increased to 904,313. See more statistics on this topic at http://nccsdataweb.urban.org

Providing needed services, non-profits can be museums, social agencies, or humanitarian services. They are not in business to make a profit--they are in business to serve a community, a specific group of people. For instance, the Arthritis Foundation's goal is to help people with arthritis and their families. The Red Cross assists people when disaster strikes.

A non-profit organization is a business that is unable to hold or distribute profits like a "for-profit" organization. This means that non-profit organizations cannot issue or sell stock/shares. Since non-profits cannot pay dividends on any earnings and they have no owners, one cannot "invest" in non-profit organizations the same way that one can in a business. A person or business can promote certain programs by donating to a non-profit, but the expectation of getting a return on investment does not exist.

Non-profit organizations are also known as "charities," or "exempt organizations" or even "NPOs." They can be large and small. Several prominent hospitals such as Kaiser Permanente and recognized universities, such as UCLA, are set up as non-profits. Other well-known non-profits are the Better Business Bureau, Carnegie Corporation of New York, and the New York State Society of CPAs.

Non-profit organizations can also be religious orders, churches, and trade organizations. Usually, if a non-profit organization has a website, you can recognize it by the ".org" at the end of the website address. In the case of educational institutions, you may see the ".edu" instead.

Non-profits can be seen as an extended arm of government in the sense that many receive government funding to supply services that "big government" cannot provide. Often, government has programs, but it cannot really deliver the needed services. For example block grants for social services are usually distributed to social agencies/non-profits that can do the work.

Many non-profits are based in the U.S. but operate worldwide. Organizations, such as the Red Cross, Doctors without Borders and International Medical Corps conduct a lot of its charitable work outside the U.S. Because of the complexity, many organizations' employees are very knowledgeable about foreign treatises, laws, etc. I personally witnessed the case of a charity worker being jailed in Africa and the officials in the U.S. having to deal with the situation. It was challenging, to say the least. The charity worker ended up all right because officials knew how to handle these kinds of situations.

Some countries don't have non-profits and others, such as the United Kingdom, have non-profits but they are not called "non-profits," they are called "charities" only. These charities have to be registered with the Charity Commission of that country.

In the U.S, a non-profit organization is a business entity that has received an exemption from the IRS, so that it does <u>not</u> need to pay income taxes. This business entity provides needed services within a community. Many rules and regulations apply in this area to prevent fraud and abuse.

Most non-profits are corporations which requested exemption status from the IRS after being formed. Non-profits come in a wide variety of code sections. Some common types from the IRS website: <u>www.irs.gov</u>

- 501(c)(1)  Corporations created by Congress such as Federal Credit Unions
- 501(c)(2)  Title holding corporations for exempt organizations. Usually used limited for non-profits to own real estate and collect funds
- **501(c)(3)  Assorted charitable, non-profit, religious, and educational organizations, including many hospitals. The 501 (c) (3) in general is the main focus of this publication.**
- 501(c)(4)  Various political education organizations
- 501(c)(5)  Labor unions and agriculture,
- 501(c)(6)  Business league and chamber of commerce organizations
- 501(c)(7)  Recreational club organizations

- 501(c)(8)  Fraternal beneficiary societies
- 501(c)(9)  Voluntary employee beneficiary associations
- 501(c)(10)  Fraternal lodge societies
- 501(c)(11)  Teachers' retirement fund associations
- 501(c)(12)  Local benevolent life insurance associations, mutual irrigation and telephone companies, and like organizations
- 501(c)(13)  Cemetery companies
- 501(c)(14)  Credit unions
- 501(c)(15)  Mutual insurance companies
- 501(c)(16) Corporations organized to finance crop operations
- 501(c)(17)  Employees' associations
- 501(c)(18) Employee-funded pension trusts created before June 25, 1959
- 501(c)(19)  Veterans' organizations
- 501(c)(20)  Group legal services plan organizations
- 501(c)(21)  Black lung benefit trusts
- 501(c)(22)  Withdrawal liability payment fund
- 501(c)(23) Veterans' organizations created before 1880
- 501(c)(25) Title-holding corporations for qualified exempt organizations
- 501(c)(26)  State-sponsored high-risk health coverage organizations
- 501(c)(27) State-sponsored workers' compensation reinsurance organizations
- 501(c)(28)  National railroad retirement investment trust

501(c) is a specific provision of the United States Internal Revenue Code (26 U.S.C. § 501(c)) that relates to non-profit organizations, also known as "exempt organizations."

In order to become an exempt organization under section 501(c) (3), form 1023, depending on the type of charity, must be filed with the IRS within twenty-seven months of the corporation creation with proper fees.

The IRS has plans to release "Cyber Assistant" software to help with the application process in 2010. Organizations filing form 1023 using the system will pay reduced fees: www.irs.gov.

Note that other documentation, such as Federal Employer ID and Power of Attorney, is required by the IRS. At the state level, other forms may be necessary as well.

After the initial request for tax exemption is approved, (form 1023) the IRS sends the organization a form letter 1045, a favorable 501(c)(3) determination letter indicating an Advance Ruling in favor of the organization. This is good news. The 1045 letter shows the time the Ruling begins (usually the date the corporation was formed) and when it will end -- five years in the future. Even though it is a temporary letter, you can give this letter to donors and they can deduct their donations. It will take five years to get the "permanent" letter from the IRS indicating that the organization is indeed non-profit/exempt.

What do you do after getting the 1045 letter?

It is time to plan ahead. Review form 8734, to be filed five years later to confirm exempt status. In order to properly fill out this form, the organization needs to keep track of money donations, donations of things, and expenses paid by someone else on the organization's behalf, etc. Make sure to start compiling this information. The point is to show on form 8734 that the organization is publicly supported.

If all goes well, the organization should get a form letter 1050 from the IRS. This is the favorable letter issued when the review of Advance Ruling financial data indicates that the organization meets the applicable public support tests. This is the famous "Final Determination Letter." Make sure to make several copies of this letter and to keep it safe. The IRS doesn't provide duplicates. The best the IRS does later is to confirm that the organization is tax exempt, which is usually accepted, but it is better to retain the original determination letter.

See the next pages for examples of the letter 1045, form 8734, and 1050 letter.

INTERNAL REVENUE SERVICE
TE/GE Division 4900 DEN
1244 Speer Blvd., Suite 442
Denver, CO 80204-3583

DEPARTMENT OF THE TREASURY

Date:   JAN 3 0

Employer Identification Number:

DLN:

Contact Person:

Contact Telephone Number:

Accounting Period Ending:
    June 30
Foundation Status Classification:
    509(a)(1)
Advance Ruling Period Begins:
    September 14, 2000
Advance Ruling Period Ends:
    June 30, 2005
Addendum Applies:
    No

Dear Applicant

Based on information you supplied, and assuming your operations will be as stated in your application for recognition of exemption, we have determined you are exempt from federal income tax under section 501(a) of the Internal Revenue Code as an organization described in section 501(c)(3).

Because you are a newly created organization, we are not now making a final determination of your foundation status under section 509(a) of the Code However, we have determined that you can reasonably expect to be a publicly supported organization described in sections 509(a)(1) and 170(b)(1)(A)(vi).

Accordingly, during an advance ruling period you will be treated as a publicly supported organization, and not as a private foundation. This advance ruling period begins and ends on the dates shown above.

Within 90 days after the end of your advance ruling period, you must send us the information needed to determine whether you have met the requirements of the applicable support test during the advance ruling period. If you establish that you have been a publicly supported organization, we will classify you as a section 509(a)(1) or 509(a)(2) organization as long as you continue to meet the requirements of the applicable support test. If you do not meet the public support requirements during the advance ruling period, we will classify you as a private foundation for future periods. Also, if we classify you as a private foundation, we will treat you as a private foundation from your beginning date for purposes of section 507(d) and 4940.

Grantors and contributors may rely on our determination that you are not a private foundation until 90 days after the end of your advance ruling period. If you send us the required information within the 90 days, grantors and contributors may continue to rely on the advance determination until we make

Letter 1045 (DO/CG)

10

a final determination of your foundation status.

If we publish a notice in the Internal Revenue Bulletin stating that we will no longer treat you as a publicly supported organization, grantors and contributors may not rely on this determination after the date we publish the notice. In addition, if you lose your status as a publicly supported organization, and a grantor or contributor was responsible for, or was aware of, the act or failure to act, that resulted in your loss of such status, that person may not rely on this determination from the date of the act or failure to act. Also, if a grantor or contributor learned that we had given notice that you would be removed from classification as a publicly supported organization, then that person may not rely on this determination as of the date he or she acquired such knowledge.

If you change your sources of support, your purposes, character, or method of operation, please let us know so we can consider the effect of the change on your exempt status and foundation status. If you amend your organizational document or bylaws, please send us a copy of the amended document or bylaws. Also, let us know all changes in your name or address.

As of January 1, 1984, you are liable for social security taxes under the Federal Insurance Contributions Act on amounts of $100 or more you pay to each of your employees during a calendar year. You are not liable for the tax imposed under the Federal Unemployment Tax Act (FUTA).

Organizations that are not private foundations are not subject to the private foundation excise taxes under Chapter 42 of the Internal Revenue Code. However, you are not automatically exempt from other federal excise taxes. If you have any questions about excise, employment, or other federal taxes, please let us know.

Donors may deduct contributions to you as provided in section 170 of the Internal Revenue Code. Bequests, legacies, devises, transfers, or gifts to you or for your use are deductible for Federal estate and gift tax purposes if they meet the applicable provisions of sections 2055, 2106, and 2522 of the Code.

Donors may deduct contributions to you only to the extent that their contributions are gifts, with no consideration received. Ticket purchases and similar payments in conjunction with fundraising events may not necessarily qualify as deductible contributions, depending on the circumstances. Revenue Ruling 67-246, published in Cumulative Bulletin 1967-2, on page 104, gives guidelines regarding when taxpayers may deduct payments for admission to, or other participation in, fundraising activities for charity.

Contributions to you are deductible by donors beginning September 14, 2000.

You are not required to file Form 990, Return of Organization Exempt From Income Tax, if your gross receipts each year are normally $25,000 or less. If you receive a Form 990 package in the mail, simply attach the label provided, check the box in the heading to indicate that your annual gross receipts are normally $25,000 or less, and sign the return. Because you will be treated as

Letter 1045 (DO/CG)

a public charity for return filing purposes during your entire advance ruling period, you should file Form 990 for each year in your advance ruling period that you exceed the $25,000 filing threshold even if your sources of support do not satisfy the public support test specified in the heading of this letter.

If a return is required, it must be filed by the 15th day of the fifth month after the end of your annual accounting period. A penalty of $20 a day is charged when a return is filed late, unless there is reasonable cause for the delay. However, the maximum penalty charged cannot exceed $10,000 or 5 percent of your gross receipts for the year, whichever is less. For organizations with gross receipts exceeding $1,000,000 in any year, the penalty is $100 per day per return, unless there is reasonable cause for the delay. The maximum penalty for an organization with gross receipts exceeding $1,000,000 shall not exceed $50,000. This penalty may also be charged if a return is not complete. So, please be sure your return is complete before you file it.

You are not required to file federal income tax returns unless you are subject to the tax on unrelated business income under section 511 of the Code If you are subject to this tax, you must file an income tax return on Form 990-T, Exempt Organization Business Income Tax Return. In this letter we are not determining whether any of your present or proposed activities are unrelated trade or business as defined in section 513 of the Code.

You are required to make your annual information return, Form 990 or Form 990-EZ, available for public inspection for three years after the later of the due date of the return or the date the return is filed. You are also required to make available for public inspection your exemption application, any supporting documents, and your exemption letter. Copies of these documents are also required to be provided to any individual upon written or in person request without charge other than reasonable fees for copying and postage. You may fulfill this requirement by placing these documents on the Internet. Penalties may be imposed for failure to comply with these requirements. Additional information is available in Publication 557, Tax-Exempt Status for Your Organization, or you may call our toll free number shown above.

You need an employer identification number even if you have no employees. If an employer identification number was not entered on your application, we will assign a number to you and advise you of it. Please use that number on all returns you file and in all correspondence with the Internal Revenue Service.

This ruling is based on the understanding that the majority of your Board of Directors will be non-salaried and will not be related to salaried personnel or to parties providing services. It is also based on the understanding that salaried individuals cannot vote on their own compensation and that compensation decisions will be made by the board.

This determination is based on evidence that your funds are dedicated to the purposes listed in section 501(c)(3) of the Code. To assure your continued

Letter 1045 (DO/CG)

exemption, you should keep records to show that funds are spent only for those purposes. If you distribute funds to other organizations, your records should show whether they are exempt under section 501(c)(3). In cases where the recipient organization is not exempt under section 501(c)(3), you must have evidence that the funds will remain dedicated to the required purposes and that the recipient will use the funds for those purposes.

If you distribute funds to individuals, you should keep case histories showing the recipients' names, addresses, purposes of awards, manner of selection, and relationship (if any) to members, officers, trustees or donors of funds to you, so that you can substantiate upon request by the Internal Revenue Service any and all distributions you made to individuals. (Revenue Ruling 56-304, C.B. 1956-2, page 306.)

Evidence you submitted with your application shows that you may engage in lobbying activities. Section 501(c)(3) of the Code specifically prohibits lobbying as a substantial part of your activities. If you do not wish to be subject to the test of substantiality under section 501(c)(3), you may elect to be covered under the provisions of section 501(h) of the Code by filing Form 5768, Election/Revocation of Election by an Eligible Section 501(c)(3) Organization to Make Expenditures to Influence Legislation. Section 501(h) establishes ceiling amounts for lobbying expenditures.

If we said in the heading of this letter that an addendum applies, the addendum enclosed is an integral part of this letter.

Because this letter could help us resolve any questions about your exempt status and foundation status, you should keep it in your permanent records.

If you have any questions, please contact the person whose name and telephone number are shown in the heading of this letter.

Sincerely yours,


Director, Exempt Organizations

Form 872-C

Letter 1045 (DO/CG)

# Support Schedule for Advance Ruling Period

Please refer to the separate instructions for assistance in completing this schedule. For additional help, call IRS Exempt Organizations Customer Services toll free at 1-877-829-5500.

OMB No. 1545-1836

For tax years beginning _____, and ending _____, 20___

| Print or type. See Specific Instructions. | Name of organization | | Employer identification number |
|---|---|---|---|
| | Number and street (or P.O. box number if mail is not delivered to street address) | Room/Suite | Telephone number ( ) |
| | City or town, state, and ZIP + 4 | | E-mail address _____ Fax number ( ) |

**Note:** ? Get **Schedule A (Form 990 or 990-EZ)**, *Organization Exempt Under Section 501(c)(3), and its separate Instructions before you complete this form.*

? *If you did not receive any support for a given year, show financial data for the year by indicating -0- or none.*

? *Year 1 should reflect support received as of the date legally organized, unless otherwise specified in the determination letter.*

? *Organizations that filed Form 990 or 990-EZ will be able to use information reported on Schedule A, Part IV-A, to complete this form.*

| Calendar year (or fiscal year beginning in) | (a) Year 5 | (b) Year 4 | (c) Year 3 | (d) Year 2 | (e) Year 1 (See Note above.) | (f) Total of Years 1 through 5 |
|---|---|---|---|---|---|---|
| 1 Gifts, grants, and contributions received. (Do not include unusual grants. See line 14.) | | | | | | |
| 2 Membership fees received | | | | | | |
| 3 Gross receipts from admissions, merchandise sold or services performed, or furnishing of facilities in any activity that is related to the organization's charitable, etc., purpose | | | | | | |
| 4 Gross income from interest, dividends, amounts received from payments on securities loans (section 512(a)(5)), rents, royalties, and unrelated business taxable income (less section 511 taxes) from businesses acquired by the organization after June 30, 1975 | | | | | | |
| 5 Net income from unrelated business activities not included in line 4 | | | | | | |
| 6 Tax revenues levied for your benefit and either paid to you or expended on your behalf | | | | | | |
| 7 The value of services or facilities furnished to you by a governmental unit without charge. Do not include the value of services or facilities generally furnished to the public without charge | | | | | | |
| 8 Other income. Attach a schedule. Do not include gain (or loss) from sale of capital assets | | | | | | |
| 9 Total of lines 1 through 8 | | | | | | |
| 10 Line 9 minus line 3 | | | | | | |
| 11 Enter 1% of line 9 | | | | | | |

For Paperwork Reduction Act Notice, see page 6 of separate instructions.

Cat. No. 10010S

Form **8734** (Rev. 1-2004)

**12**  If you are an organization that normally receives a substantial part of your support from a governmental unit or from the general public, complete lines **12a** through **12f**. (Sections 509(a)(1) and 170(b)(1)(A)(vi)). **If you want the IRS to compute your public support test as a section 509(a)(1) and 170(b)(1)(A)(vi) organization, complete only lines 12a and 12b.**

| | | |
|---|---|---|
| **a** Enter 2% of amount in column (f), line 10 . . . . . . . . . . . . . . . . . . . . . . . . . . . . . . . . . . . | **12a** | |
| **b** Attach a list showing the name of and amount contributed by each person (other than a governmental unit or publicly supported organization) whose total gifts for Year 5 through Year 1 exceeded the amount shown in line 12a. Enter the total of all these excess amounts . . . . . . . . . . . . . . . . . . . . . | **12b** | |
| **c** Total support for section 509(a)(1) test: Enter line 10, column (f) . . . . . . . . . . . . . . . . . . . . . . . . . . . . | **12c** | |
| **d** Add: Amounts from            45 _____    _____ | | |
|    column (f) for lines:          8 _____    12b _____ . . . . . . . . . . . . . . . . | **12d** | |
| **e** Public support (line 12c minus line 12d total) . . . . . . . . . . . . . . . . . . . . . . . . . . . . . . . . . . | **12e** | |
| **f Public support percentage (line 12e (numerator) divided by line 12c (denominator))** . . . . . . . | **12f** | % |

**13**  If you are an organization that normally receives: **(1) more than 33$\frac{1}{3}$%** of your support from contributions, membership fees, and gross receipts from activities related to your exempt functions, and **(2) no more than 33$\frac{1}{3}$%** of your support from gross investment income and net unrelated business taxable income from businesses acquired by the organization after June 30, 1975, complete lines **13a** through **13h**. (Section 509(a)(2)). **If you want the IRS to compute your public support test as a section 509(a)(2) organization, complete only lines 13a and 13b.**

**a**  For amounts included in lines 1, 2, and 3 that were received from a "disqualified person," attach a list showing the name of, and total amounts received in each year from, each "disqualified person." Enter the sum of such amounts for each year:

(Year 5) . . . . . . . . . . . . . (Year 4) . . . . . . . . . . . . . (Year 3) . . . . . . . . . . . . . (Year 2) . . . . . . . . . . . . . (Year 1) . . . . . . . . . . . . .

**b**  For any amount included in line 3 that was received from each person (other than "disqualified persons"), attach a list showing the name of, and amount received for each year, that was more than the **larger** of **(1)** the amount on line 11 for the year or **(2)** $5,000. (Include in the list organizations as well as individuals.) After computing the difference between the amount received and the larger amount described in **(1)** or **(2)**, enter the sum of these differences (the excess amounts) for each year:

(Year 5) . . . . . . . . . . . . . (Year 4) . . . . . . . . . . . . . (Year 3) . . . . . . . . . . . . . (Year 2) . . . . . . . . . . . . . (Year 1) . . . . . . . . . . . . .

| | | |
|---|---|---|
| **c** Add: Amounts from column (f) for lines:   1 _____   2 _____ | | |
|                                 3 _____   6 _____   7 _____ . . . . . . . . | **13c** | |
| **d** Add: Line 13a total _____ and line 13b total _____ . . . . . . . . . . . . . . . | **13d** | |
| **e** Public support (line 13c total minus line 13d total) . . . . . . . . . . . . . . . . . . . . . . . . . . . . . . . . | **13e** | |
| **f** Total support for section 509(a)(2) test: Enter amount from line 9, column (f) . . .  \|**13f**\| | | |
| **g Public support percentage (line 13e (numerator) divided by line 13f (denominator))** . . . . . . . . . . | **13g** | % |
| **h Investment income percentage (line 4, column (f) (numerator) divided by line 13f (denominator))** | **13h** | % |

**14**  **Unusual Grants:** For an organization described in line 12 or 13 that received any unusual grants during Year 5 through Year 1, attach a list showing for each year the name of the contributor, the date and amount of the grant, and a brief description of the nature of the grant. **Do not include these grants in line 1.**

**List the amount of unusual grants excluded for each year below.**

(Year 5) . . . . . . . . . . . . . (Year 4) . . . . . . . . . . . . . (Year 3) . . . . . . . . . . . . . (Year 2) . . . . . . . . . . . . . (Year 1) . . . . . . . . . . . . .

**15**  Please list the name and telephone number of an officer, director, or trustee who can be contacted during business hours if we need more information. If someone other than an officer, director, or trustee will represent the organization, attach a properly completed **Form 2848**, Power of Attorney.

Name: _____
<br>Type or print name and title.

Phone: ( ) _____        Fax Number (if available): ( ) _____

| Please<br>Sign<br>Here | I declare under the penalties of perjury that I am authorized to sign this form on behalf of the above organization and that I have examined this form, including the accompanying attachments, and to the best of my knowledge it is true, correct, and complete. | |
|---|---|---|
| | Signature of officer, director, or trustee | Date |
| | Type or print name and title or authority of signer | |

15

INTERNAL REVENUE SERVICE                    DEPARTMENT OF THE TREASURY
DISTRICT DIRECTOR
2 CUPANIA CIRCLE
MONTEREY PARK, CA 91755-7406

                                            Employer Identification Number:
Date:        Mar 06 1996
                                            Case Number:

                                            Contact Person:

                                            Contact Telephone Number:

                                            Our Letter Dated:
                                               May 17, 1991
                                            Addendum Applies:
                                               No


Dear Applicant

        This modifies our letter of the above date in which we stated that you would
be treated as an organization that is not a private foundation until the expiration
of your advance ruling period.

        Your exempt status under section 501(a) of the Internal Revenue Code as an
organization described in section 501(c) (3) is still in effect. Based on the
information you submitted, we have determined that you are not a private foundation
within the meaning of section 509(a) of the Code because you are an organization of
the type described in section 509(a)(1) and 170(b)(1)(A)(vi).

        Grantors and contributors may rely on this determination unless the Internal
Revenue Service publishes notice to the contrary. However, if you lose your section
509(a) (1) status, a grantor or contributor may not rely on this determination if he
or she was in part responsible for, or was aware of, the act or failure to act, or
the substantial or material change on the part of the organization that resulted in
your loss of such status, or if he or she acquired knowledge that the Internal
Revenue Service had given notice that you would no longer be classified as a section
509(a) (1) organization.

        If we have indicated in the heading of this letter that an addendum applies,
the addendum enclosed is an integral part of this letter.

        Because this letter could help resolve any questions about your private
foundation status, please keep it in your permanent records.

        If you have any questions, please contact the person whose name and telephone
number are shown above.

                            Sincerely yours,




                            District Director




                                                        Letter 1050 (DO/CG)

Note that an organization formed under the code 501(c) (3) cannot participate in political activity, including endorsing any candidates for public office. An organization may promote legislation; however, if a significant amount of time is spent in lobbying activities, it could lose its tax-exempt status. Lobbying is allowed up to a certain point.

In this book, we will discuss the basic structure of the non-profits, accounting issues, types of revenues, grants, and financial statements. We will also cover taxation (Gasp! taxation for non-profits? Yes.), internal controls, and special considerations of non-profits you may not be aware of, such as pension plans and risks.

# CHAPTER 3

## *TYPICAL STRUCTURE OF NON-PROFITS*

*"Men love to organize."*

James Mooney (1884-1957 U.S. business executive)

Non-profits and for-profit organizations may look the same on the surface. They both provide goods and services, they may charge people, they may provide classes, etc. But there is one main difference – <u>Non-profits are NOT interested in making a profit.</u>

The non-profit's goal is to provide a public service, not to enrich owners. Actually, ownership does not exist in the non-profit world. However, someone "minds the store." There are stakeholders. For instance, a board of directors oversees the organization; donors are interested in seeing that their donations are well spent; and banks are interested in the non-profit's viability and ability to pay back loans.

There is a structure to the organization to ensure that it runs effectively. Many non-profits have a President, Vice-Presidents, maybe a CFO, and/or a Controller. Larger organizations may have "chapters," like branches and a headquarter office. Programs are offered to the public and an administrative office manages overall operations. Non-profits need to be very well managed to survive within the financial and other constraints of the sector, especially in tough economic times.

The two major types of non-profit organization structure are membership and board-only. A membership organization elects the board and has regular meetings and power to amend the bylaws. The main issue with this type of non-profit is the complexity of the Model Non-profit Corporation Act's requirements on membership decision making. (The Model Non-profit Corporation Act is legislation prepared by the American Bar Association committee that states use to govern non-profit corporations. It mandates many procedures that are different from standard parliamentary procedure.)

A board-only organization usually has a self-selected board, and a membership whose powers are limited to those delegated to it by the board. An example of such a structure is the American Society of Association Executives.

## Operational Areas

Any business needs a structure to operate effectively, and non-profits are no different. A non-profit organization's business is to provide goods and services to a community, following its mission statement. Similar to for-profits, non-profits try to operate with a method and within budget. It is crucial for non-profits to run efficient operations and to demonstrate measurable outcomes, because they are accountable to donors, board members, and the government.

As in any business sector, there is a need for an effective infrastructure working behind the scenes to keep things running smoothly. This is especially true in the non-profit sector where operations support the organization in a number of functional areas, including office management, accounting and finance, administration, human resources, information technology, and development/marketing. Across all of these functional areas there is one objective: to make sure the organization is operating efficiently and to its full potential in providing goods and services to a community.

One of the challenges of non-profits is to create and manage a structure that works well. Many founders of non-profits are not managers and do not have a background in management. They are "program" people. They created the non-profit to fulfill a goal, a dream that they are familiar with, but management is not their expertise.

It is important for founders and boards of directors to realize this issue and to find proper personnel to fill out the needed spots. I have seen new, small organizations fail to follow their mission statements because they didn't have a basic infrastructure, management, personnel to deal with proper insurance, and other risk factors.

A common structure is for non-profit operations to be divided into three areas, all supervised by the board of directors. (Note that tax returns and most financial reports are classified by these three areas.)

- **Programs/ Services**
- **Management and General**
- **Fundraising**

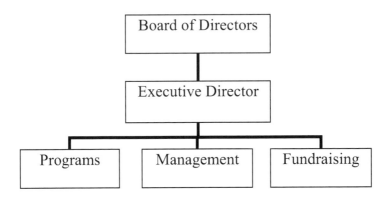

## Programs/Services

As discussed earlier, non-profit organizations are set up to provide programs and goods/services. Programs are the heart of any non-profit organization. If a non-profit provides no programs or services, then there is no reason to exist. If the purpose of an organization is to help the homeless, the non-profit will offer programs in accordance with this goal. Most likely programs would involve temporary housing, food distribution, and job training.

It is important to identify programs as such. For instance, an organization could sell used clothes in a thrift shop. The thrift shop is most likely part of the fundraising area and not the program. However, what if the organization provides job training for teens? Then, the thrift shop may be part of a program, especially if it has teens working there, being trained in the shop's operations and selling techniques.

The first step in identifying programs is to look at the organization's mission statement. A good, clear mission statement is critical. The clearer and simpler the mission statement, the easier it is to identify major programs--the reasons for the organization to exist.

Suppose a non-profit's mission statement is to "provide temporary shelter to the homeless." It is simple and focused. If the organization hosts a car race, then it is not part of a program--most likely it is part of fundraising.

An organization with the mission statement "helping people to become self-sufficient" is too general, increasing the chances of confusion about what is a program and what is not. The more focused the mission statement, the easier it is to identify programs versus other operational areas. It makes it easier for the organization to stay on track, as well.

Why is it so important to identify programs? Because organizations report on programs. Donors want to know that their donations are going mostly to programs and not to fundraising. Identification of the three main areas of non-profit operations, including programs, is crucial to set up proper accounting systems, internal controls, reporting, and management.

If you want to research non-profit organizations, including programs, Guidestar is for you. It is a comprehensive online database with over 1.5 million organizations, including information about mission statements, financial information, and even copies of tax returns. Users can use it for free for basic information. You can reach it at www.guidestar.org

*The mission statement is so important that the tax form 990 specifically requests the mission statement, right in front!*

Measuring a program's success is a challenge for many organizations. Donors (and grantors) want to know if programs are working and if they should continue funding. Some programs are short-term and attendance can be a sign of success. This could be the case in a hotline program, where the number of calls received is a good measuring stick.  If the hotline is to help people with referrals for babysitting, then the number of kids placed would be more indicative of success.

To ensure that the future success of a program is measurable, people involved in delivering programs must be trained in getting proper documentation for reporting and gauging success.

As programs are set up, the question, "How can we show that the program works?" should be kept in mind. A baseline may be created to compare "before" and "after." Programs should have measurable goals, such as to serve 200 families, or to provide food for 100 homeless people. If a program has the goal of improving the mental health of 100 men, then there must be a way to measure not only the number of men, but also to measure improvements within these men. These measurements could be observation by clinicians or running of tests on the men.

An important area in programs is government grants. Grants are given to organizations for specific programs and a percent of expenses is used for overhead/indirect costs. Many grant makers, including the government, have their own measuring methodology to gauge program success. Review grant contracts carefully.

Another concern of non-profits within the program area is its expenses. According to the Jewish proverb, *"If charity cost nothing, the world would be full of philanthropists."* Programs do not run for free. Program expenses can be classified as direct and indirect. Employees may work for various programs, or just for one. An art program has more art supply expenses than a sports program. A night program may involve more security expenses than a day program. There are no hard and fast rules in this area, but art supplies being expensed as part of a night program that has nothing to do with art may raise some eyebrows.

Allocating expenses to programs and other areas can be a challenge. Donors/grantors are interested in expense allocations to make sure they are not paying for personal expenses and other non-authorized uses of the money. If a foundation was funding the night program mentioned above, it may ask for reports and would make inquiries about the art supplies being charged to that program. Large grantors, such as governments, usually impose their own methodology on identification and application of program expenses.

Accounting systems should be able to identify and report on program expenses. This is usually done through the chart of accounts, which keeps program expenses separately from other areas. Many non-profits also keep expenses separated by program, with not all programs mixed in one account. Supply expenses from Program A would be separated from supply expenses from Program B.

Not surprisingly, the program area usually reports the most expenses in financial statements. Since programs are the reason for the organization's existence, this area is carefully reviewed by donors and grantors. They wonder how much of the total expenses was actually spent on programs. 80 percent? 25 percent? The higher the percentage, the better off the organization is in the eyes of donors and grantors.

## Management and General

Per Peter Drucker, *"Management is doing things right; leadership is doing the right things."* This is what management is about: leadership doing the right things right.

The "management and general" area is composed of all items not directly related to programs or to fundraising. This area is also known as "General and Administration," or G&A. G&A provides the background for all the other sectors to function effectively.

Non-profit management has the challenge of keeping the organization fiscally viable, of hiring the right people for many jobs, and overall oversight of operations. Usually, the management and general area consists of:

- Planning and strategy--both long term and short term
- Accounting /finance activities, including budget preparation and reporting
- Human Resources processes--hiring and keeping the right people, employees' benefits
- Risk management--insurance issues, safety
- Legal issues--dealing with lawsuits and other legal matters
- Construction oversight and management

- Building maintenance
- IT--computer and software purchases and upkeep
- Safety of assets
- Investment decisions

An interesting duty of management is to assess in-kind donations--donations of things--before they are accepted. A donation of land or a building may at first seem to be great, but then, upon closer look, the organization may be responsible for cleaning up hazardous materials, etc. It is usually management's responsibility to accept donations that make sense to the organization. For instance, a non-profit may not be able to accept a work of art because it cannot afford insurance in it. Development staff may be able to determine if the in-kind donation is acceptable or not, but most often I have seen G&A personnel performing this function.

Management decisions could be made by employees or by volunteers, depending on the organization. Large expenses are often reviewed by board of directors. If an organization needs to conduct major renovation or construction, usually board members are involved in the management of the project.

Nowadays, without proper management and overview, organizations may not survive. Donors want a sense of security and they want to trust management in doing the right things. Reputation is important. A well-managed organization is effective and efficient, and donors appreciate that.

One of the issues I have seen in this area is about administrative decisions made by committees and not by a person. Some decisions are to be made by committee, but many are forced into committee because nobody wants to take responsibility for the decision. This can be time-consuming and not in the best interests of the organization. If an executive is supposed to make a decision and he/she cannot, then something is wrong. It could be that the organization needs to hire people with the right background, let the executive go, or maybe the person trying to make the decision is not the right one within the organization. The committee process of decision making is not effective or efficient in many cases, especially when the committee is made up of people not qualified to make the decision.

For example, an organization was implementing a new nationwide system for donations. Nobody at the executive level had the experience or the knowledge to make decisions about it. Next, a committee was set up of employees at different levels to make major decisions about the new system. Up to a certain point, committee decisions were valid and made sense. However, the organization really needed a Chief Information Officer to oversee this process and to make sound decisions in this area.

Another challenge of the G&A area is about donors, especially foundations and wealthy individuals, refusing to donate for G&A. They want their money to go to a specific cause or research. Their reluctance in allocating funds for G&A (also known as overhead) is due to the fear of abuse by executives, partly because of too many scary stories in the media about these cases.

Psychologically, it is more heartwarming to donate to a specific program, rather than to donate to general operations of an organization.

The end result is that organizations are required to use other funds to cover G&A expenses. Many times galas and other fundraising efforts are to cover G&A/overhead. This problem has reached a crisis point in many non-profits, where funds are restricted for programs only and nothing can be used for management. As we know, without management, the non-profit cannot properly fulfill its mission and programs. Basically, the non-profit may close if it only has program-restricted funds.

With difficult economic conditions, some organizations "borrow" funds from restricted programs to other areas. Some states may not allow this and it looks odd in financial statements. Borrowing and not repaying may be a sign that the non-profit may close or may be merged with another one soon. This is not a long–term strategy that works.

Currently, many non-profits require donors to stipulate a portion of grants to G&A and overhead, or they cannot accept the grant. Some places require that at least 10 percent of donations over a certain amount to be allocated toward G&A. This is a very hot area within non-profits these days.

The G&A area usually reports the second highest expense amount in financial statements, after programs.

## Fundraising

Fundraising is also known as "Development" in the non-profit world. The closest counterpart of this in the for-profit world would be "Marketing." While for-profit marketing's goal is to increase sales, development's goal is to increase donations/grants.

Fundraising/Development staff markets the organization, searches for funding sources, and monitors amounts received. Fundraisers plan and work on fundraising activities, such as a golf tournaments, dinner parties, or telethons. They could also write grant proposals for foundations, businesses, and governments. Many times, development people set up seminars about the virtues of donating and how to include the non-profit in wills and as part of estate planning.

A non-profit is not in business for fundraising. It should not be the most important goal of the organization, but the non-profit needs to survive and to maintain its programs. Fundraisers are a necessity to maintain current funding and to find other sources of funding, including business and government grants.

The fundraising department's goal is to make the organization's programs attractive to donors, who could be individuals, foundations, businesses, governments, or other non-profits. Often, it is about selling a new program, or improving or changing existing ones. Maybe the organization needs to purchase computers--who would be interested in donating to this cause? Maybe the organization needs to obtain more funds to help the increasing homeless population--who would be interested in this cause?

The Development department creates brochures and marketing materials to sell the organization to prospective donors and grantors. They can make presentations, set up radio and TV spots, etc.

Many times, board members are the best fundraisers for the organization. Larger non-profits may have a Director or VP of Development and an entire department dedicated to raise funds. In other organizations, this function is outsourced.

Many grantors, especially government, do not pay for fundraising expenses. Paying development people based on a percentage of amount donated is a bad idea. The Association for Fundraising Professionals specifically prohibits this in its ethics code:

"Members shall not accept compensation or enter into a contract that is based on a percentage of contributions; nor

shall members accept finder's fees or contingent fees."
http://www.afpnet.org

Some non-profits give bonuses to fundraisers when they meet certain thresholds, but not a percentage of money raised. Be aware that states and cities may have different laws about fundraisers and fundraising. Many require registrations or permits and other paperwork filed.

Make sure that expenses related to fundraising make sense and that events actually raise more funds than is spent. Fundraisers may not take into consideration the overhead costs of conducting a fundraiser event, or payroll costs. Sometimes fundraisers are not aware of sales taxes some states apply on special events or auctions.

> *An organization conducting raffles or bingo or other games of chance should file a form W2-G with the government if the winnings are for $600 or more. Check out Publication 3079 at the IRS site, www.irs.gov.*

Nowadays, donations can be received from websites. Make sure the website is user-friendly and interesting to attract and retain donors. The website must be easy to navigate with contact information (phone number and e-mail address) and the ability to receive funds online through outfits such as PayPal, which is easy to set up and is reasonably priced.  Posting pictures of contacts and something personal about them can create a fuzzy feeling and make people more likely to contact and donate.

The latest trend in fundraising is "mobile giving," or giving through texting.  Never underestimate the power of technology. Alicia Keys, the famous musician, asked people to dial a number and text "ALIVE" during one of her concerts. More than 8,000 did during the concert, raising about $40,000 for AIDS. As the artist put it, "Texting can provide a way to give at that instant when we are moved, rather than later when life takes over."
http://non-profit.about.com

Accepting donations should be very easy.  If donors cannot find the right person, or cannot find information about the organization, they may go someplace else with their donations. Be flexible, accept credit card donations, and be ready to help out willing donors. Work with donors' employers, who may match donations of employees. Donors should feel welcome by everyone in an organization, not just by development personnel. Many times donors call the accounting department or other departments to make donations over the phone. Make sure everyone is trained to be gracious and thankful.

Non-profit organizations are a vital sector of our economy, providing social services, humanitarian work, scientific, and educational venues to help society.  Most non-profit operations can be broken down into the areas of program, general and administrative, and fundraising. Program is the most important area for any non-profit and it defines what the non-profit does and why it exists. While G&A provides the backbone for the organization's programs, fundraising is important to maintain and grow the organization. All areas are grounded in the mission statement, the reason for the organization to exist.

# CHAPTER 4

## *ACCOUNTING BASICS*

*"Money is better than poverty, if only for financial reasons."*

Woody Allen

Non-profits need money to survive. Good deeds can carry an organization only so far. And with money, comes accounting for it. Since non-profits are not in the business of making a profit, accounting differences between for profits and non-profits warrant some discussion.

A good way of looking at it is to assume that accounting for non-profit organizations is the same as for-profits, but with an extra level of detail. It is similar to project accounting. Revenue is not just revenue. Revenue could be related to a specific program or to a grant. The source and kind of revenue need to be tracked. By the same token, expense is not just an expense. Is it supposed to be reimbursed? Is it a general expense? Is it supposed to be allocated? Is it supposed to be funded by more than one source? Expenses are tracked in a very detailed manner.

Most accounting concepts that apply to for-profits also apply to non-profits. GAAP (Generally Accepted Accounting

Principles) is followed and includes the same ideas, but with a twist. There are differences in reporting and an extra step in booking both revenues and expenses. The Financial Accounting Standards Board (FASB) and other organizations provide guidance in this sector.

Accounting for non-profits is also known as "fund accounting." The word "fund" means different things to different people. For our purpose in this publication, funds and net assets are meant to be the same thing. Many years ago, "funds" could be set up regardless of being unrestricted or not. The concept then was much looser than now, where "funds" are used to segregate categories of revenues received.

Currently, the main purpose of fund accounting (non-profit accounting) is the stewardship of financial resources received to be spent in compliance with legal or other requirements. It is not about investors' interests; it is about having adequate funds/net-assets to provide for present and future programs and services.

In order to accommodate the detail level, accounting systems are set up with many digits in the accounting "code" or "ID." Accounts are set up to identify revenue/expense types, fund types, and grantors. It is not unusual to see at least eight digits in the accounting code. For example, 7800.44.782.002--the first four digits identify an expense account, the "44" is a department, "782" is a funding source and "002" identifies the fund. Some non-profits use a project module to help with the details and reporting.

It is important to identify funds and to recognize accounts belonging to an unrestricted fund versus a restricted fund. For instance, "002" could be a restricted fund in an accounting code. All accounts with these digits in a segment belong to a restricted fund, with no exceptions. It gets VERY confusing when the same segment or the same code is used for more than one purpose.

I have seen a situation where segments were used haphazardly and it became impossible to easily identify unrestricted fund accounts from restricted ones. Instead of fixing the chart of account, reports were set up to pick up certain accounts known to belong to one fund or another. This setup worked up to a certain point, but then more accounts were added to the chart of accounts and they were not being picked up by the report. The result was not pretty; fund balances were wrong in all reports.

Please look at the section about chart of accounts for a more detailed discussion on this topic.


## Cash or Accrual

Per GAAP, the accrual method should be used for non-profits. The reality is that many small organizations use cash basis or modified cash, and at year-end, the books are adjusted for accruals.

The main advantage of the cash basis of accounting is that it reflects the current cash situation. Revenues shown are revenues actually received. Expenses shown are expenses actually paid. Often board members and management prefer cash basis reports with separate information on current payables and receivables. They want to know if current funds are sufficient to conduct an event, to cover a major unexpected expense, or to meet payroll responsibilities.

Many board members don't understand accrual reports and may get really confused in the accrual basis. For example, many do not comprehend that $1 million showing as revenue in the financials may not really have been received. This can get more confusing if receivables are long-term, covering more than one year, but recognized in the present. The revenue will show up once, but the money will be received and used in the future. Be aware that many board members do not understand GAAP accounting or any accounting at all. Reports need to be flexible to accommodate Board needs.

Cash basis is conservative in recognizing revenues. If large pledges are not collectible, cash basis may provide a more realistic view of the financial situation of the organization.

Cash basis accounting has inherent weaknesses, such as not recognizing future revenues or expenses. This makes planning difficult. For instance, if the organization is supposed to pay $100,000 within the next few months, it is better to show this liability now in one single report and not be surprised later on. Maybe this expense is in the budget, maybe not. If this were an unexpected liability, it may not have been budgeted for it at all.

Another weakness of the cash basis of accounting is timing. Revenue recognition is not on the same timing as expenses. The timing is off and it may create confusion. Suppose an organization has a paid expense of $100,000 and a receivable/revenue for the same amount. Using the cash basis, financials show a loss, when in fact, there is no loss. This is misleading.

Cash basis wouldn't be appropriate if a non-profit is trying to measure the cost of a program and bills are received and paid in the future. Expenses may be "forgotten," especially if they show up months later. One would need to wait until all bills are received and paid to get a good idea of the cost of a program.

Sometimes, especially if there are no receivables, differences between cash and accrual basis are not material. Organizations may be in cash basis and then adjustments can be made for reporting purposes with no major consequences.

There are many good reasons for the non-profit to report on accrual basis, rather than on cash basis. Not only is accrual accepted by GAAP, but also by IFRS, International Financial Reporting Standards (IFRS), standards and interpretations adopted by the International Accounting Standards Board (IASB). The IFRS may not have much effect now on non-profits, but it is just a matter of time before it will start trickling down to the non-profit sector.

If an organization has substantial receivables/revenue and is in the accrual basis, a receivables aging report would be useful. Maybe only $100,000 was collected and that would be valuable information to management.

Example of a report using cash versus accrual basis (The Statement of Financial Position is the non-profit's version of a balance sheet.)

The Do-good organization
Statement of Financial Position/Statement of Assets and Liabilities Resulting from Cash Transactions.
December 31, 20X1

|  |  |  | Cash Basis |
| --- | --- | --- | --- |
| Assets |  |  |  |
|  | Cash |  | 10,000 |
|  | Interest receivable |  | 0 |
|  | Pledges receivable |  | 0 |
|  |  |  |  |
| Total Assets: |  |  | 10,000 |
|  |  |  |  |
| Liabilities |  |  |  |
|  | Accrued expenses |  | 0 |
|  |  |  |  |
| Net Assets |  |  | 10,000 |

This report shows that accrued expenses are significant to the organization and this organization would benefit by using the accrual basis of accounting. If this organization is using the cash basis, then a list of expenses and due dates would be helpful.

# Funds

A "fund" is also known as a "net asset" in the non-profit sector. "Fund" may have a different connotation than "net asset," but for the purpose of this publication, they will mean the same thing. Fund/Net asset is a basic entity for a non-profit organization. In the for-profit world, we have retained earnings. In the non-profit world, we have funds or net assets.

All business transactions of a non-profit must be booked in a fund. A fund is like a project. Each revenue and expense must be booked in a specific fund, not just in an account. It must be an account within a fund. For instance, if a non-profit has $100 in postage expense, the question is not just which account this expense should be booked to, but also which fund or grant it relates to. If there are departments, then the expense needs to be booked in the right account, department, and fund. As noted earlier, normally non-profit organizations' accounts have many digits to identify regular accounts, departments, grants, and funds.

Revenues and expenses are closed to the fund they relate to. <u>Expenses and revenues are NOT closed into retained earnings.</u> They are closed in the fund they belong to. For example, suppose a donation was made for a program in the future, the following year. The revenue will be booked in an account in the temporarily restricted fund, say 4000-01-003. At period-end, the balance in the account will close in the temporarily restricted fund and not in the unrestricted fund.

Once the books are closed, typically non-profits have three fund/net asset balances:
- ✓ Unrestricted Net Assets
- ✓ Temporarily Restricted Net Assets
- ✓ Permanently Restricted Net Assets

If someone gives a non-profit $10,000 to be used within three years, a non-profit needs a mechanism to identify this money and to spend it properly. This can be a challenge, because once funds are closed, there are only ending balances "visible." It is important to keep documentation and historical data to support funds that are to be spent in the future. In the for-profit world, similar items would be booked as deferred revenues. Not in the non-profit world.

Some organizations meet this challenge by having many restricted sub-funds, one for each purpose. Others keep historical spreadsheets on what each fund or sub-fund contains. Many do both. It is too easy to "forget" funds received. Be aware of this simple and common problem–very characteristic of non-profits.

Because of the detail level required in restricted fund accounting, a "roll-forward schedule" is a common report in many non-profits. This is a schedule showing beginning balances of all funds, any transactions and the ending balance in the funds. Next is an example of this type of schedule:

| Roll Forward - Restricted funds worksheet for year 2005 | | | | |
|---|---|---|---|---|
| Segment # | Beg. Balance | Increases | Decreases | End. Balance |
| 503 Scholarship Fund | 100,000 | 40,000 | (15,000) | 125,000 |
| 504 Book Fund | 50,000 | 3,000 | (1,000) | 52,000 |
| 509 Building Fund | 125,000 | - | (30,000) | 95,000 |
| Total Restricted | 275,000 | 43,000 | (46,000) | 272,000 |

The ending balance in the schedule should agree with the restricted fund balance in the general ledger. Increases in funds could be donations. Decreases could be related to expenses (See "Release of Net Assets" covered later on).

Some non-profits keep separate checking accounts for each fund and reconcile the balance on each fund with the books at least once a year. The point is not to forget about funds and not to spend them inappropriately. Suppose that restricted funds from the example earlier are kept in a separate savings account in the bank. Suppose that interest from the savings account is to be used in the unrestricted fund. At year end, if interest was transferred to an unrestricted cash account, the balance per bank and the balance per books-restricted funds should be the same. Chances for money to be misspent are minimized.

Real life scenario: A non-profit received $60,000 from a donor to buy academic books. A couple of years later this donor asked the organization what books were purchased with the funds. The organization didn't keep good records and really didn't know where the money went. It was not a pretty picture to see the accounting and development departments stumbling around to get information. Needless to say, the donor was not pleased.

Restricted funds must be considered when budgeting for a non-profit. There may be certain expenses that may be covered by those, but are "forgotten" in the restricted fund.

## Fund Types

Funds/net assets are an intrinsic part of non-profit accounting. They provide structure for the organization to identify and to keep track of different types of donations/grants.

There are three main types of funds:
- General fund or unrestricted net assets
- Restricted fund or temporarily restricted net assets
- Permanently restricted fund or permanently restricted net assets

Funds are created to segregate resources, which could be limited by law, donors, government, or board wishes. SFAS 117, promulgated in 1993, gives official guidance on this topic. The idea is to identify and report on funds and not bunch them all together. SFAS 117 provides rules of what is booked in each fund.

Funds/Net assets are NOT assets. They can be thought of as projects with their own financial statements. When books are closed, revenue and expenses are closed in different funds, as if each project has its own "private" retained earnings. For example, a non-profit has $200 in temporarily restricted revenues and $300 in unrestricted revenues. The $200 would be closed in the temporarily restricted net assets and the $300 would be closed in unrestricted net assets. Both are net assets, but one is restricted to be used in the future and the other one is not.

Net assets can be understood as assets less liabilities, or the formula:

**ASSETS= LIABILITIES + NET ASSETS**

Example of Balance Sheet version for non-profits:

Organization do-best
Statement of Financial Position
December 31, 20xx

| Assets | | | |
|---|---|---|---|
| | | Cash | xx |
| | | Accounts Receivable | xx |
| Total Assets | | | xx |
| | | | |
| Liabilities | | | |
| | | Payroll payable | xx |
| | | Accounts payable | xx |
| Total Liabilities | | | xx |
| | | | |
| Net Assets | | | xx |
| Total Liabilities and Net Assets | | | xx |

Instead of Retained Earnings, the "Net Assets" line is usually presented separately in three lines:

Net Assets:
| | |
|---|---|
| Unrestricted Net Assets | xx |
| Temporarily Restricted Net Assets | xx |
| Permanently Restricted Net Assets | xx |

Typically, funds/net assets are presented as columns in the Statement of Activities (Income statement for non-profits). Next is an excerpt of this statement:

The Helping organization
Statement of Activities
Year ended December 31, 20x1

| | | Unrest. fund | Temp. Restricted fund | Perm. Restricted fund | Total |
|---|---|---|---|---|---|
| Revenue | | | | | |
| | Contrib. | 100,000 | 50,000 | 20,000 | 170,000 |
| | Fees for serv. | 55,000 | | | 55,000 |
| | ~ | ~ | ~ | ~ | ~ |
| | ~ | ~ | ~ | ~ | ~ |
| | ~ | ~ | ~ | ~ | ~ |
| Ending Net asset Balance | | 250,000 | 50,000 | 20,000 | 320,000 |

The example shows that $50,000 is to be recognized in the future and is being presented as the balance of Temporarily Restricted funds. $20,000 was contributed to the permanently restricted fund. Most of the contributions, $100,000, were booked in the unrestricted fund to be used in general, daily activities.

## General Fund-Unrestricted Net Assets

This fund is used to run operations, day-to-day activities, and general transactions of the organization. It is also known as *"Unrestricted"* or *"Current Unrestricted Fund"* or *"Operating Fund."* This fund contains resources that are not restricted. All general donations are booked in this fund. This fund could be the only one used on all activities, if an organization has no restrictions on donations. Revenues and expenses from general fundraising events are booked into this general fund.

A non-profit may receive $10,000 to be used for current activities. How is this transaction recorded? The amount is booked in the unrestricted fund. The entry would be a debit to cash and a credit to revenue-contributions-unrestricted fund.

Revenues for a specific activity not part of general operations, such as construction of new facilities, are <u>not</u> booked into this fund. This type of revenue is booked in a temporarily restricted fund. It is restricted for construction only.

Most expenses run though the general fund, even though revenues are booked in another fund. For example an organization receives $5,000 to be spent in clothes for a homeless program only. Accounting staff debits cash and credits a temporarily restricted account. Once the $5,000 is spent, then a credit is made to cash and a debit is made to clothes expense- <u>unrestricted</u>. Another journal entry is done using the "Net Assets Released from Restriction" to decrease the temporarily restricted fund and to credit the general fund. The end result is that expenses are shown in the unrestricted fund, but are credited out with a journal entry. The "Net Assets Released" account will be discussed in more detail later on.

An interesting sub-set of the general fund is the Board Designated Fund. Boards can designate funds to pay for certain items. An example would be a "generosity fund" set up by the board for specific programs. The board could also change its mind and use the funds for something else. That's why this type of fund is part of the general fund "umbrella" and not restricted funds. Boards cannot restrict funds, only donors can.

Unrestricted funds can be important if the non-profit has a debt covenant, such as loans or bonds. Many banks require a minimum balance in the unrestricted fund as part of the loan or bond deal.

## Restricted Fund-Temporarily Restricted Net Assets

This fund is also known as *"Donor Restricted Fund"* or *"Temporarily Restricted Fund."* This fund is to be used for a specific purpose, as per the donor's wishes. Board of directors cannot override a donor's wishes. If a donor wants the money to go for brain cancer research only, board members cannot override this wish and apply the funds toward publications, for instance, without express consent of the donor.

Not surprisingly, organizations should exercise due-diligence to spend funds in accordance with donors' express desires. Written documentation to justify the restriction is a must. If the donor doesn't want to put anything in writing, the organization could send a "thank you" note confirming the donor's desires.

Donors can restrict funds for a specific activity, program, event, etc. But there are limits. Many non-profits have policies about what amounts and objectives can be restricted in the accounting books. These policies should be made public. What if a donor wants to donate $100 to something that doesn't exist? Should a new restricted fund be opened? Is it feasible? What is the policy of the organization in this regard? Is it public knowledge? Is this transparent? The answers to these questions should be a resounding "yes."

Organizations may have various temporarily restricted funds, such as for "scholarships" and any moneys for any scholarships are booked there. Funds set up should be functional enough to accommodate most of the restricted funds.

A major restricted activity may involve several stages. This is the case of a capital campaign for construction. Some donors want to donate after construction has started, while others would like to donate for a specific room or classroom. In this case, separate sub-accounts within the temporary fund capital campaign "umbrella" could be set up.

Many times the donation is for use in the future and the restriction is about time and actual expenses. Once the restriction is lifted, revenue is considered to be unrestricted and it is "released."

For example, a donor gives $10,000 to defray expenses of a travel program for a school. The $10,000 is booked in the restricted fund and then, as travel expenses occur, revenue is released from temporarily restricted to the unrestricted fund. Once the organization occurs $10,000 in travel expenses, the balance in the restricted fund would be zero.

Sometimes donations are to be used in the future because of a special event and expenses don't matter. For example, a donor gives $5,000 to commemorate a tenth anniversary. On the day of the anniversary, the amount is released regardless of expenses.

Restricted funds can be classified as restricted by time only and by expenses. When funds are used to cover expenses, the overall net effect is zero. When funds are used up because of timing only, there is an increase in the unrestricted fund without any expenses related to it; the net effect is NOT zero. The unrestricted fund will increase.

Net assets can be released up to the balance in the restricted funds. When a non-profit has only unrestricted funds, then there is no need to release anything. If a restricted fund has a net asset balance of $20,000, then releases can be made up to $20,000 only. Balances on restricted net assets cannot be negative.

Overall, restricted fund balances should decrease as expenses are booked, net assets released and/or as time progresses, depending on the restriction. The idea is for all temporarily restricted funds to be used up.

## Permanently Restricted Fund- Permanently Restricted Net Assets

Many people leave money to charity in their names or names of their families. They want to be remembered after they are gone. In order to give and to be remembered "in perpetuity," usually donors want the principal balance of the donation to remain intact, while the organization can use up income or gains / losses associated with it. These moneys are booked into a permanently restricted fund, also known as "endowment fund." This fund is held in perpetuity or for a very long time and principal cannot be used. Usually, endowment funds are large and many are given out after a person dies because of a will. Sometimes wealthy families with foundations also give gifts as "endowments."

It is important to have a written document specifying the details of the donation, any restrictions, and where to apply gains/losses/income, etc. In many cases, when the stock market and other investments lose value, such as during a recession, organizations may have large endowments, but may not be able to use it. Many organizations are facing this dilemma in 2009.

More information on how non-profits are dealing with the economic downturn can be found in this Wall Street Journal's article: http://online.wsj.com/article/SB123432521248071761.html. (If the link is no longer available, you may need to search within the wsj.com site.)

Sometimes organizations may need to go to court to be able to access the funds held in the endowment, if the state permits.

Usually, the larger the endowment fund, the stronger the organization's financial situation. Colleges are known for having large endowments. Harvard University had an endowment of about $34.6 billion in 2007. With the latest recession, endowments have lost value and many are "underwater," that is, the current value is less than the original amount.

Many states adopted UPMIFA (Uniform Prudent Management of Institutional Funds Act), providing uniform and fundamental rules related to investments and expenses related to endowments.  Check your state laws on endowments. Some states allow for an inflation/deflation effect on investments.  Some do not.

# Inter-fund Accounts

Inter-fund accounts are accounts that link all funds. They are zeroed out at consolidated level when all funds are presented. For instance, a general fund may need to borrow from restricted funds to meet current obligations. That creates a liability in the general fund and a receivable in restricted funds. Many times due to/due from accounts are used to keep track of who owes what to whom.

For example, some small equipment for a restricted program was purchased using cash from the general fund. Restricted funds are kept in another bank. An inter-fund receivable is set up for the unrestricted fund and an inter-fund payable is setup for the restricted fund. Once a check is written from a restricted to unrestricted cash account, this journal entry is reversed.

Expenses are presented in the unrestricted fund, as discussed earlier. Instead of using the expense accounts in the restricted fund, the unrestricted fund accounts are used.

So, how do we show "expenses" in the restricted fund? How do we decrease the balance of the restricted fund? By using net assets released from the restrictions account.

## Net Assets Released from Restrictions

This account is normally used between the unrestricted fund and the temporarily restricted fund. It is reported in the revenue area of financial statements as one line item. This account is one of the different areas between non-profits and for-profits. The concept does not exist in the for-profit sector.

The "net assets released from restrictions" account mechanically decreases restricted expenses in the unrestricted fund, making it a "wash" with zero consequences for the unrestricted fund.

For example: Organization A paid $500 for literacy books. Literacy book donations are kept in a restricted fund. Cash for the expense came out of the general fund checking account. The journal entries would be:

JE-1GF-Literacy book expense     500
         GF-Cash                              500


JE-2GF- Inter-fund receivable     500
         RS- Inter-fund payable            500

**JE-3RF-Net assets released from restriction  500**
         **GF-Net assets released from restriction        500**

GF=General fund
RF=Restricted fund

The first journal entry books the transaction in the General Fund. Usually this entry is made in the Accounts Payable module, as the check is processed.

The second journal entry books the inter-fund receivable and payable because the money for this expense was deposited in the restricted fund cash account and now is coming out of the general fund cash account. Once cash is transferred from one banking account to another, this entry is reversed. Cash transfers may occur once a month or every quarter based on balances on inter-fund accounts.

The third journal entry recognizes the transaction as restricted. The release from restrictions entry "reclassified" the expense from the general fund to the restricted fund. The end-result for the organization using the "net assets released from restriction" is zero. However, the restricted fund is decreased.

If restricted revenue becomes unrestricted because of timing issues, the revenue can be released from restricted funds. For example, let's say that $10,000 is to be used only after someone's birthday, which happens today. The organization has had this amount on the books since 2001 and only now can it be used to commemorate this birthday. The Journal entry will be:

RF-Net assets released from restriction          10,000
              GF-Net assets released from restriction     10,000

Actual cash can be transferred as well. Or an inter-fund receivable/payable can be set up.

It is important to know why something is being released. Some organizations keep releases from restriction in a separate spreadsheet with details, while others prefer to add to the description of the account or transaction. Auditors want to know if funds were released properly. Donors may not be interested in the mechanics of fund release, but want to have assurances that things are going according to their plans.

When funds are released, they may not be available for future unrestricted expenses. This is a common misunderstanding. Funds may be released because expenses already occurred. The release is basically an accounting concept, "covering" the unrestricted fund for its expenses with restricted fund. When funds are released on the account only because of time, then funds indeed may be available for future expenses. Because of this issue, keeping track of types of restriction is important for budgeting and planning.

Many non-profits book expenses directly into each fund, even if it is against 117. This makes it easier to present restricted transactions. Instead of booking expenses in the unrestricted fund, they are booked in the restricted funds directly, so the board and others will know that an expense happened and for what purpose. It is not just a debit from the release account. Non-profits can use non-GAAP reporting internally and then they can make adjustments to comply with SFAS 116-117, or they may make adjustments for final annual reports only and not in the books per se.

> *If adjustments are made only at the report level, then the total net asset released should agree with the total expenses in restricted funds.*

Next is an example of a "rogue" organization booking adjustments at year-end for its annual audited report:

Transactions:
1-Organization paid $4,000 for specific therapy covered by a restricted fund--Using cash from the *general fund.*
2-Organization paid $10,000 for specific therapy covered by a restricted fund--Using cash from a *restricted fund.*
Journal entries:

| | | |
|---|---|---|
| 1-a-RF Therapy expense | 4,000 | |
| GF Cash | | 4,000 |
| 1-b-GF- Inter-fund receivable | 4,000 | |
| RF Inter-fund payable | | 4,000 |
| | | |
| 2- RF Therapy expense | 10,000 | |
| RF Cash | | 10,000 |

Note that this "rogue" organization does not use the "Release from temporary restrictions" account on a regular basis.

At year-end, adjustments were needed to make these transactions conform to SFAS 116-117 by moving all expenses to unrestricted fund/net assets, etc:

1-a -GF Therapy expense             4,000
     RF Therapy expense             4,000
To reclassify expense to General fund


**1-b-RF Net assets released from restriction      4,000**
    **GF Net assets released from restriction   4,000**
**To book release of restrictions**


2-a-GF Therapy expense             10,000
     RF Therapy expense             10,000
To reclassify expense to General Fund

**2-b-RF Net assets released from restriction      10,000**
    **GF Net assets released from restriction  10,000**
**To book release of restrictions**

As you may note, the effect in the unrestricted fund is a "wash" -- zero. Expense was booked there, but a credit for the same amount was booked there as well.

Some organizations keep track of restricted and unrestricted funds on a monthly basis, others do it quarterly, and many do it at the end of the year. Some non-profits have a policy that if funds are to be used in the current year, then the money is booked in unrestricted funds the entire year.

## Chart of Accounts

The chart of accounts should be able to accommodate funds, inter-fund receivables/payables, and reporting for financials and 990 purposes. The chart of accounts should also accommodate grant reporting. Many organizations set up their chart of accounts following the line items in the 990 and that is usually good enough. But many times Board of Directors' reporting can be more detailed. So, be careful in this area. If the chart of accounts is messed up, it is quite painful to fix it later on.

When setting up chart of accounts, segments should be thought about carefully. It is common for non-profits' chart of accounts to have many segments to account for type, department, event, or program and fund.

The common reporting needs of non-profits require the chart of accounts to be multi-dimensional and to allow for reports by program, department, grant, funds, etc.

Comprehensive Example:   Non-profit organization A has three programs: Therapy, Tutorial Services, and Child Care. It receives funds from a government grant and from public donations.

The organization uses the setup XXXX- YYYY

Fund ID
1-General
3-Temp.Restricted
5-Permanently Rest.

Dept/Program ID
1-Therapy
2-Tutorial
3- Child Care

Assets:

1001-1000- Cash Unrestricted
1001-3000- Cash Temporarily Restricted
1001-5000- Cash Endowment
1002-5000- Investment-Endowment

Accounts Receivable:

1010-1000-Accounts Receivable-Unrestricted
1010-3000-Accounts Receivable-Restricted
1050-1000-Interfund Receivable-Unrestricted
1050-3000-Interfund Receivable-Restricted

Liabilities:
2000-1000-Accounts Payable-Unrestricted
2000-3000-Accounts Payable-Restricted
2050-1000-Inter-fund Payable-Unrestricted
2050-3000-Inter-fund Payable-Restricted

Net Assets/Funds:
3000-1000-General/Unrestricted Fund
3000-3000-Temporarily Restricted Fund
3000-5000-Permanently Restricted Fund

Revenues:

4000-1000-General contributions

4005-1100-Contributions for Therapy-Unrestricted
4005-1200-Contributions for Tutorial-Unrestricted
4005-1300-Contributions for Childcare-Unrestricted
(*All three unrestricted accounts above to be used if organization wants to separate contributions. Otherwise, they could ALL be booked in the general contribution account 4000-1000*)

4090-1000-Net assets released from restriction (*usually a credit*)
4090-3000-Net assets released from restriction (*usually a debit*)

4100-1100-Fees for services-Therapy
4100-1200-Fees for services-Tutorial
4100-1300-Fees for services-Child Care

4200-3100-Contributions-Therapy-Restricted
4200-3200-Contributions-Tutorial-Restricted
4200-3300-Contributions-Child Care-Restricted

4300-1001- Annual fundraising event
4301-1001- Contra revenue account to account for donor's direct costs of event

Expenses
6000-1000-Salary-Administrative
6000-1100-Salary-Therapy

6000-1200-Salary-Tutorial
6010-1000-Telephone-Administrative
6010-1100-Telephone-Therapy
6010-1200- Telephone-Tutorial
*(Note that all expenses are coming out of unrestricted fund)*

Using this setup, reports can be generated by fund, by program, by type of account, etc. The last two digits of the second segment can identify different fund raising events and special programs within each department. For instance, within the therapy department, we could separate therapy for teens and therapy for adults. The more detailed the chart of account is, the more flexible it is in reporting. (Therapy for teens and adults could also be segregated by using a project module or even "classes," as available in some software products.)

If this organization receives a $1,000 donation for any purpose, then account 4000-1000 is credited. This account closes into General Fund balance/net asset-3000-1000.

If someone donates $2,000 to be used in therapy to start next year, then account 4200-3100-Contributions-Therapy-Restricted is credited. This account closes into the 3000-3000-Temporarily Restricted Fund. This could be the case also if the $2,000 is to fund a specific type of therapy not yet available.

Suppose that $2,000 was to defray costs of therapy or other costs in general, then this money could be booked in the account 4005-1100-Contributions for Therapy-

Unrestricted. It will be closed in the general fund 3000-1000.

- All income/expense accounts like XXXX-1YYY- close into 3000-1000
- All income/expense accounts like XXXX-3YYY- close into 3000-3000
- All income/expense accounts like XXXX-5YYY- close into 3000-5000

Chart of accounts should be set up for users to compile data for both financials and 990 tax returns. There could be other reports to donors, sales tax on certain sales, fundraisers' reports, etc. There is a fine line between having an effective chart of accounts and one that is too cumbersome to maintain.

Keep in mind that many grants and restricted funding cover more than one fiscal year and reports may be required for periods not following the regular fiscal year. I have seen grants run for two years, from May to April, and reporting for those was quite a bear. Unless an organization has a project/grant module, a big part of the reporting has to be done manually, taking lots of time and resources.

Accounting for non-profits can be confusing for many, even experienced professionals. The use of net-assets, the release of restrictions--these are concepts related to the non-profit sector only. Many non-profits have issues with their chart of accounts and management may not be aware of this. Sometimes management decides to keep the original chart of accounts, changing instead the reporting mechanism. I highly recommend going to the heart of the problem and changing the chart of accounts, instead of playing around with reporting, which could miss new accounts.

# CHAPTER 5

## *TYPES OF REVENUE*

*"May your charity increase as much as your wealth."*

Proverb

All businesses must have some kind of revenue to survive and pay its bills. Unlike for-profit businesses where revenue streams come from sales or billings, non-profit organizations' revenues come from donations, gifts, and grants.

Non-profit organizations receive many different types of income. Some non-profits are government funded, while others get funds from donors and foundations. Many are funded in multiple ways.

*Since when are donations tax deductible? Congress passed the income tax deduction for charitable contributions in 1917, four years after ratification of the Sixteenth Amendment, which set up the federal income tax.*

The main source for guidance in this area is SFAS 116-
*Accounting for Contributions Received and Contributions
Made.* See full text at http://www.fasb.org/ All other SFAS
noted in this chapter can be found at this web address.

Unlike for-profits, not all revenues are "Sales" or "Services."
Many types of revenue have strings attached.

## Regular Donations/Contributions

Not-for-profit organizations receive donations from people,
businesses and foundations. An example of this type of
donation is when you make a general donation to your
charity, or the charity makes appeals of general nature.

A regular donation is when a donor doesn't receive
anything in return for the donation--not tickets, baked
goods, or anything else. It is NOT for a dinner or a dance. It
is NOT payment on a trip bought at an auction. These types
of donations are discussed under "Fundraising" later on in
this chapter.

A regular donation is one where a donor makes a payment
and gets nothing in return (except for receipts, thank you
letters or cards).

# Donations of Cash/Checks

Suppose a donor gives a $10,000 check to Do-Good charity. This was a regular donation to be used for any purpose. The journal entry for this transaction will be :

GF-Cash  10,000
            GF-Revenue 10,000

GF= General fund

Suppose another donor gives $20,000 to Do-Good charity. This was for a specific program to start in the following year and it was deposited in a restricted cash account. The journal entry will be:

RF-Cash 20,000
            RF-Revenue 20,000

RF=Restricted fund

The restricted fund revenue account is credited whether the cash was deposited in the restricted cash account or not. Note that a Deferred Revenue account is not used. The restricted revenue account will be closed into a Restricted Fund/Net asset account.

The disadvantage of this setup is that once the revenue is closed to restricted fund, details on the fund may be "lost."

Regarding the example above, the $20,000 will be closed into the restricted fund balance and may "get lost" there. Three years from this year's close, the charity may not know what the money was for. So, maintain good records for all restricted funds accounts. Otherwise, the books may show a balance of $100,000 in the restricted fund years from now, and nobody would know what this balance was for.

Policies on revenues should be very clear and specific. Accounting staff must review fundraising literature going out to make sure that when donations are received, the accounting staff know where to book the funds.

I have seen marketing materials going out without a space for credit card expiration dates. I also have seen donation cards going out allowing people to donate to certain funds that do not exist; maybe the restricted funds were created many years ago and were closed, but the donation cards were never changed. So, before any campaign or marketing material goes out, someone from the accounting staff should look at it.

Revenues can also be generated by fees charged in programs (usually unrestricted money) and by unrelated business activities. The unrelated business activity is carried on by the non-profit, but it is taxed as regular income for-profit business revenue. More information about this topic is available in the tax section of this publication.

*Tax form 990 asks specifically on Part VIII to report revenue from all sources. Look at this part to identify revenue types by line item. Your chart of accounts should accommodate this reporting.*

See next an example of revenue being reported on a Statement of Activities (Income Statement for non-profits) with $50,000 received as restricted for future use. $40,000 was released in the current year, most likely a release because of timing, because there are no expenses adding up to this much in the unrestricted fund. The Do-Good Organization received $70,000 in unrestricted funds ($60,000 + $10,000) .

The Do-Good Organization
Statement of Activities
For Year Ended Dec 31, 20x1

|  | | | Unrestricted | Temporarily Restricted | Permanently Restricted | Total |
|---|---|---|---|---|---|---|
| Revenues | | | | | | |
| | Contributions | | 60,000 | 50,000 | | 110,000 |
| | Other Income | | 10,000 | | | 10,000 |
| | Net assets released from restriction | | 40,000 | (40,000) | | - |
| Total Revenues | | | 110,000 | 10,000 | - | 120,000 |
| Expenses | | | | | | |
| | Program A | | 1,000 | | | 1,000 |
| | Program B | | 3,000 | | | 3,000 |
| | Management and General | | 1,000 | | | 1,000 |
| | Fund Raising | | 500 | | | 500 |
| Total Expenses | | | 5,500 | - | - | 5,500 |
| Change in net assets | | | 104,500 | 10,000 | - | 114,500 |
| Net assets at the beginning of the year | | | 12,000 | 5,000 | | 17,000 |
| Net assets at the end of the year | | | 116,500 | 15,000 | - | 131,500 |

# Stock donations-securities

Non-profits may receive stocks as donations. Many people donate appreciated stock donations to non-profits to avoid paying taxes on gains. These are especially popular in December.

In order to safeguard the stocks or to cash them, an organization needs to work with a brokerage firm that can hold the actual stocks or sell them.

Stock donations are booked as assets. FASB released SFAS 124, *Accounting for Certain Investments Held by Not-for-Profit Organizations,* bringing consistency on how to account for investments by non-profits. Under SFAS 124, non-profits are supposed to:

1. Report at current fair value any equity investments that have readily determinable fair values; and
2. Show any gains or losses in the Statement of Activities, one of the standard financial statements.

Many non-profits have an investment committee that decides how to invest funds and monitor fund performance. Usually non-profits are conservative in investment strategies and work with independent brokers.

Often, non-profit organizations have policies about stock donations. Some hold on to the stocks, some sell it right away, some leave the decisions to their brokers based on certain parameters or goals.

Suppose stocks are given to fulfill pledge commitments. It is important to get the fair market value of the stock when given to verify if proceeds would fulfill the commitment or not. Actual funds received may be more or may be less than pledges. Donors will need to be contacted about directions on how to apply any surplus and/or how to pay outstanding commitments in full.

Non-profits give receipts for stock values when donated for donors' tax returns. Any gains or losses, dividends, etc. are to be booked by organizations as investment transactions.

If securities were donated with no restrictions, any gains or losses are booked into the unrestricted fund. If the securities were given as restricted and the donor gave specific instructions on gains and losses, donor wishes should be followed. Realized and unrealized gains and losses are booked the year they happen and in the fund/net asset they belong to.

Example:

1- An organization receives an equity security valued at $30,000 in year 20X1
2- At fiscal year-end, the value of the security is $40,000
3- The organization sells the security for $43,000 in year 20X2

The security is booked as an investment. Unrealized gain of $10,000 is recognized at 20X1 year end. In year 20X2, realized gain of $3,000 is booked by the organization, along with cash of $43,000.

Donations of stocks could be given as part of a permanent restricted fund. Endowments' income and gain/losses could be booked to temporarily restricted funds, unrestricted, or permanently restricted funds, depending on the donor's stipulation and local law.

The case of investment losses is interesting because donor endowment funds are supposed to stay static and not lose value. However, if losses go beyond the gains booked in other funds, then the endowment fund could absorb the loss (assuming this treatment is allowed by law and donor).

It all depends on how the endowment was written and what stipulations the donor had. This is a controversial area, especially in times of stock losses. Be careful not to be stuck with worthless stocks and to be sure to protect the organization in case of stock losses.

Some endowments are specific on the type of investment to be held and managed, and the manner income, gains, and losses are to be applied. This avoids confusion later on. The more specific a donor is, the better the organization can account for the endowment.

If a non-profit receives significant stock donations and it has the ability to influence a firm's financial and operating policies, then the equity method of accounting is to be used.

This is handled the same way as if the non-profit were a for-profit firm.

Be aware of FASB 157, *Fair Value Measurements*, regarding investments' valuation and monitoring, especially if the non-profit has alternative-type investments that are inherently riskier. Be aware of UPMIFA, discussed earlier.

## Pledges Receivable

Most non-profit organizations are familiar with pledges. People, businesses, and foundations can make pledges to donate in the future. Pledges are basically promises to give. Many times pledges are the result of a fundraising campaign or an appeal. Depending on the situation, the pledge could be for a general purpose, or for a specific purpose, such as a new child-care program.

People can make promises to pay an amount every year, or at a certain period in time. Pledges receivable could be unrestricted or restricted. They could be short-term or long-term receivables. Many times board members are required to make pledges to be allowed on the board.

SFAS 116, *Accounting for Contributions Received and Contributions Made,* requires that all unconditional pledges be recorded as assets.

For instance, a donor pledges $2,000 a year for five years: this is an unconditional gift. The pledge is booked as a receivable (asset) and revenue the date the pledge is received.

Suppose there is a condition associated with a pledge. The pledge is recorded only after the condition is met. For example, a donor pledges $10,000 if there is a major disaster in California. This pledge is conditional and shouldn't be recorded. Once a disaster hits California, then the pledge is valid.

Another example of a condition is for a firm to match donations made by employees. If an employee donates $10, the firm would also pay $10, matching the donor's amount. As the employee donates, the condition on the firm's pledge is lifted. So, each time an employee pays, a matching pledge is recognized in the books.

The key word in conditional pledges is "if." The wording of a pledge is crucial to determine if a promise is conditional or just restricted. Usually, unconditional restricted pledges use "when" or "what," not "if."

A pledge can be restricted to a certain time or event, such as for a reading program that will happen in the future. This is a temporarily restricted pledge. Money will be paid, but because it is not clear exactly when the program will happen, the timing of the donation is unknown. Sometimes, donors can change their minds and instead of funding program A, they decide to fund program B. This situation happens often and proper documentation should be available to prove changes of heart.

Organizations may receive promises that are not real pledges. For example, an organization is notified that it is going to receive funds from a will. This could happen next year or in twenty years. This is not recognized as asset or revenue. The same situation exists if someone promises to pay a certain amount twenty years in the future. This is not a pledge. In both cases, donors can easily change their minds; circumstances can change, making the promises really hard to keep.

Pledges are promises and in many cases, large amounts are not collectible. Most organizations are not going to sue to collect promised amounts. So, by its nature, pledges are riskier than regular accounts receivable.

Since there is a risk of default on pledges receivable, an Allowance for Uncollectible Pledges account is used. It may be set up and adjusted every year based on history. If an organization experiences 10 percent of pledges not being collectible, then this percentage can be used. This is the same concept as the Allowance for Uncollectible Receivables in the for–profit world.

Pledges can be set up to be paid in installments, say $5,000 a year for five years. SFAS 116 requires non-profits to discount long-term pledges to present value using a reasonable percentage. The discount is amortized as it is in the non-profit world.

Pledges should be documented in writing whenever possible. If a donor does not want to acknowledge the pledge, a thank you letter confirming the pledge is a good idea. The letter can be simple and to the point, in order to leave no doubt about the existence of the pledge.

Since conditional pledges are not recognized, paperwork for this type must be filed for reference and possible follow-up.

Many times big donors want to keep their donations and personal information private. So, proper security and care should be taken so that the donor is acknowledged, donations recorded, and the donor's identity is kept private. Needless to say, donor databases must be kept secure.

Government and other grants are not considered to be pledges. Government grants are discussed in a separate chapter.

## Fundraising

Most non-profit organizations conduct fundraising events to raise money for operations or for certain programs. Often non-profits have annual fundraising events such as mailing campaigns, marathons, golf tournaments, dinners, galas, and other events to raise funds for general use. Proceeds and expenses associated with these types of events are booked in the unrestricted/general fund. If the fundraising event is for a specific program or for something to happen in the following year, then money from the event is restricted.

Usually big fundraising events are for unrestricted use. It is reported separately in the Statement of Activities-unrestricted fund column.

Many times donors get something for their donation. This is known as a "quid pro quo" and could be dinner or auctioned items, etc. Someone makes a donation and gets something in return, such as the value of food, entertainment, or items bought at an auction. This is also called "exchange value."

*Non-profits should apply for lower mailing rates.  It can make a big difference in fundraising costs.  Check out publication 417 from the IRS site, www.irs.gov*

Donors' receipts must specify how much of a donation is a "real" donation and how much is not. Donors may be able to deduct only the donation part of the gift.  If a person gives $200 for a dinner fundraiser and the ticket says "Value of the meal $50," then the donor can deduct only $150 in his taxes, not the entire amount. In an auction, if an item is valued at $1,000 and a donor pays $1,500 for it, the difference of $500 is the real donation.

If a person makes a donation for a dinner fundraiser and doesn't show up for whatever reason, s/he can deduct the entire amount. Be aware that organizations are not supposed to determine the real deductibility of an item. It can change by person and circumstances.

The IRS offers workshops to non-profits about this topic. It also has a site just for non-profit organizations at http://www.irs.gov/charities/index.html. If this link doesn't work, go to www.irs.gov .

Many times organizations combine fundraising with programs or with management/general. When that happens, a reasonable allocation of expenses may be used. Why? Because GAAP and an additional financial report, the Schedule of Functional Expenses, require this allocation. (All expenses need to be allocated to the three major areas-general/management, programs and fundraising. Also see joint costs covered in Chapter 7.)

Special events are shown separately in the Statement of Activities (Income Statement of non-profits). If the event is not that important or major, revenues and direct donor benefit costs can be shown as net. Direct donor benefits costs are direct expenses associated with the event. See below an example of reporting on a non-major special event net of direct donor benefits costs:

| Revenue | | | Unrestricted | Temporarily Restricted | Permanently Restricted | Total |
|---|---|---|---|---|---|---|
| Contributions | | | xx | xx | xx | xx |
| Special event, net of direct donor benefits of $10,200 | | | 100,500 | | | 100,500 |

Revenues and donor benefits of special events that are major and ongoing should be reported as gross--one line for revenues and one line for direct donor benefits. See below an example of a major event reporting:

| | | | | Unrestricted |
|---|---|---|---|---|
| Revenues | | | | |
| Contributions | | | | xx |
| Special event revenue | | | 110,700 | |
| Less: Cost of Direct Benefits to donors | | | (10,200) | |
| Net Revenue of special events | | | | 100,500 |

Direct donor costs could also be reported as part of expenses.

Another option for reporting major events is to use the exchange value and to divide the income between contributions and special event (see quid-pro-quo discussion). The fair market value is shown as special event revenue; the rest is shown as regular contribution.

Other items of interest regarding fundraising include the following:

1) Be sure fundraising is really bringing money in. Sometimes fundraisers do not account for all expenses included in the event. Many expenses

come in after the event. Fundraising activities should be reviewed to make sure they are indeed bringing in more than they are spending. An event bringing in $100 net of all expenses may not be worth all the work.

2) Sales/ Excise taxes- Each state has its own rules and laws regarding fundraising. Some states tax auctions, while other states tax all fundraising and yet others offer exemptions for non-profits. Taxes decrease revenues and, in some cases, it can be substantial.

3) If credit card or third parties are used in fundraising, then charges for these items must be considered. The organization may pay 3% plus as a surcharge for each donation or purchase using a credit card. When budgeting for events, take into consideration these charges.

## Revenue and Donor Receipts

The basic concept is that donations over $250 should be receipted and in the case of a quid pro quo situation, the minimum amount is $75. (Quid pro quo is when a donor gets something in exchange for the donation.)

Per the IRS (www.irs.gov), receipts for donations should have the following items:

- The donor's name

- The amount of money or a description of the item donated
- A statement indicating whether or not any goods or services were provided in return for the gift; receipts from religious organizations must include a statement indicating that "intangible religious benefits" were provided but they have no monetary value for tax purposes
- A good-faith estimate of the value of goods or services provided; insubstantial values need not be recorded

The receipt for tax purposes can be a letter, a postcard, an e-mail message, or a form created for this purpose with the name of the organization clearly shown.

Many times donors may ask for receipts for items that were not really donations. Organizations should have policies and procedures as to who is authorized to give donors receipts and for what. Non-profits don't want to participate in tax-evasion schemes and at the same time they don't want to upset a member or a donor. Clear procedures should be in place to avoid confusion and ill feelings. Sometimes the best approach is to give people general receipts for what they paid. The determination of what constitutes a donation/tax deductible would be up to the payers and their accountants.

Often, CEOs, Presidents or Executive Directors want to make the receipt more personal and they prefer to hand-write personal notes. They could have pads for receipts with the IRS information required as footers and they could handwrite a personal note on the blank space above. That way the donor would have a personalized thank you letter and an IRS receipt in one step.

Make sure to keep copies of receipts. Donors may lose original receipts and the non-profit may need to give them copies. This happens all the time, especially at tax time during the months of March and April.

As a general comment, organizations' staff should refrain from giving tax advice to donors. Every case is different and usually non-profits are not in the business of providing expert tax information. They can give the information about the event, but they cannot be held responsible for how the information is used.

Non-profits' staff should be aware of basic tax issues, but should not advise others if a donation is deductible or not. Receipts indicating that a donation is tax deductible should be avoided because each person's tax situation being different.

## In-Kind Contributions-Service Donations-Volunteers

Volunteers contribute many services to organizations. Often enough, they are the soul of an organization. Their services range from clerical work to executive positions.

Volunteering can become an important part of the organization, giving it culture and personality.

Employees are paid salaries and vendors are paid based on invoices. How does an organization account for volunteer work? Clearly there is a value to it. SFAS 116 *Accounting for Contributions Received and Contributions* provides guidance in this area.

Per SFAS 116, contributed services are recognized only if services:

- Create or enhance non-financial assets or require specialized skills
- Are provided by individuals possessing those skills, and would have to be purchased if they were not provided by donation

If either of these conditions is met, the value of services can be booked as both revenue and expense.

Doctors volunteering at a summer camp for kids with disabilities would qualify for service donations. A CPA doing an organization's tax returns for free would qualify as well.

The basis for assigning value to the services has to be reasonable. $100-$150 per hour would work for doctors or CPAs, for instance.

Fundraising volunteers are often not accounted for because they provide a financial asset: the donations.

Donated services usually have no effect on the bottom-line, since it affects both revenue and expenses. However, in some instances, because of the nature of the donation, the services could be capitalized, as in the case of volunteers working on building improvements, software programs, or another asset. Usually donated services are part of unrestricted net-assets.

Even though people's services can be recognized in the non-profit's financials, the value of services cannot be deducted from individuals' tax returns. A special mileage deduction is allowed, but people cannot deduct the value of donated services.

Donated service amounts are excluded from revenue and expenses on the 990, per IRS regulations. They can be reported in the narrative portion of the tax returns.

Volunteers' value is also important when an organization is within the first five years of existence as an exempt organization. Also, keep track of volunteers and treat them VERY well; they are promoting the organization and providing needed services.

Many organizations do not account for volunteer services because of the work involved. This is likely to change, since now the IRS asks about numbers of all volunteers.

> *Keep track of all volunteers. IRS form 990 asks about the number of ALL volunteers working at the organization. By volunteers it means all volunteers, not just professionals and others as per FASB definition. Check out the IRS site, www.irs.gov*

## In-Kind Contributions-Donations of Things

Many people and businesses donate clothes, food, furniture, jewelry, equipment, etc. to an organization. Non-profits should be careful what they accept as donations. As indicated earlier, this decision is usually made by management and it can be a challenging one.

For instance, a donor may want to donate a building and land to an organization. Should it be accepted? The answer is not until professional inspectors and other professionals give the property a clean bill of health or disclose what needs to be done to the building. Policies and procedures on this issue should include getting a professional inspection done at the donor's expense before any real estate is accepted as a gift. Maybe a major asbestos clean-up is needed, or maybe there is hazardous material underneath the soil and nothing can be done with the "gift." Sometimes gifts can cause unforeseen raises in insurance premiums, which could be prohibitive to the organization. Some gifts may require too expensive maintenance, or some other fees to keep it in working condition.

Anything of value, such as jewelry, or any item valued at $5,000 or more should be professionally inspected for value and to comply with IRS requirements. The donor fills out form 8283 and the organization fills out part IV of the form, acknowledging the gift. If the gift is sold within three years, the organization must file a form 8282 with the IRS, a copy going to the donor.

SFAS 157 *Fair Value Measurements* provides some guidance on how to measure fair value consistently for goods and services (valid both for volunteer services and for donations of things). Basically, this SFAS presents three valuation techniques that can be used alone or in combination:

> Market approach--Use market prices and other pertinent information to come up with a value
> Income approach--Use present value calculations
> Cost approach--Use replacement cost as a guide to value

http://www.fasb.org/

The organization is not required to accept every gift and it is not required to value donations. Gift valuation is usually the donor's responsibility. The non-profit can give a receipt with a detailed description of the items donated. Non-profits can use a reasonable basis to value in-kind donations for financial reporting and receipts.

## Donations of Art/Museum Pieces

Donations of antiquities and works of art are considered to be a different class of donations. These are pieces with historical or artistic value. Accounting for donations like these is covered in SFAS 116 as "Collections." Collections are art works and treasures that are:

- Used for public exhibition, research, or education, as a public service and not for financial gain
- Safeguarded, protected, and cared for
- Protected by organization policy to buy more items for collection, in case items are sold

There is a choice to capitalize the collection or not. The organization should be consistent in dealing with collections once a policy is set up. Organizations also have the choice of "grandfathering" collections before SFAS 116 and capitalizing only items acquired after adoption of SFAS 116. Capitalized collections are not depreciated.

If a collection is capitalized, it is recorded as an asset and as revenue. Collection information is shown as a separate line item in the Statement of Financial Position (the non-profit version of a Balance Sheet).

Existing collections and any other new gifts should be re-evaluated yearly regardless of the capitalization policy. The organization's insurance policy must be updated to cover any decrease or increase in value, new items, etc.

## Split Interest Agreements

Donors may want to give non-profits benefits that are shared with other parties. Sometimes a trust is used. These arrangements can be revocable or not and are called "split interest agreements." Revocable agreements are not recognized as revenue, while irrevocable ones are recognized.

Common split-interest agreements in the non-profit sector are:

- o Charitable lead trusts--Non-profit is named as beneficiary
- o Perpetual trusts held by third parties--Only income earned is distributed to the non-profit, not the assets (corpus) held in trust
- o Charitable remainder trusts--When trust terms are terminated, the non-profit receives the remaining assets
- o Charitable gift annuities--Assets are held by the organization and an annuity is set up for the third party.

- Pooled (life) income funds--Investment based on life insurance policies and funding. The donor may receive income until death, when the non-profit gets full value of the investment.

Non-profits receive many types of donations: cash/checks, promises/pledges, stocks, in-kind, and even collectibles. There are standards on how to book revenues, mostly founded in SFAS 116. The IRS guidelines are also used in this area, since the government is interested in donation receipts as far as donors are concerned. Form 990 also requests detailed information on revenue and major donors.

# CHAPTER 6

## *GOVERNMENT GRANTS*

*"The object of government in peace and in war is not the glory of rulers or of races, but the happiness of the common man."*

Lord William Beveridge (1879-1963)

The government's job is about governing, protecting, and helping people, as the saying above indicates. Part of this help is to provide services to the community. However, governments are usually too large to provide certain services to many communities. That's when non-profits come into play. Governments wouldn't be able to provide services, if it was not for the non-profit organizations they support. Government grants are the bread and butter of many non-profits.

Usually government grants involve large sums of money and grantors want assurances that funds are spent properly. Government grants can come from state, city, county, or federal sources. In this chapter we will concentrate on federal grants.

The federal government distributes large grants to states, other governments, or directly to non-profits organizations. Grants are not to be repaid. They are payments for goods and services provided by a non-profit. Interestingly, individuals and for-profit businesses can also receive government grants, such as student grants or small business administration grants. This chapter is about federal grants as they related to the non-profit sector.

A comprehensive listing of government grants can be found at the Catalog of Federal Financial Assistance at http://12.46.245.173/cfda/cfda.html. This catalog lists all federal, state, and local government grants available. There are many ways to look for grants: by keyword, agency, beneficiary type, etc. Each grant has a specific number and purpose. With the federal stimulus package, a new website was created: www.Recovery.gov.

Another good website for federal government grants is http://www.grants.gov/, containing links for non-profit organizations, offering help in writing grant proposals, and other resources.

Many non-profits function as "pass-through" entities to other non-profits. Non-profits may receive funds for research and then distribute them to appropriate institutions. The research itself is not done by the organizations, but funds are given to others, usually educational institutions involved with specific research interests.

It is important for organizations with path-through funds to get enough money to manage the grants coming in and going out. Not all is pass-through; some funds must stay within the organization to cover for direct and indirect costs associated with the management of grants.

Sometimes government entities may make non-profits the middle-man, inadvertently. A real life example: A school had been receiving government funds to distribute to disabled students via the school every month. The funds could have been sent to the families' addresses, but instead they were being sent to the school. This created an administrative burden to the school, which was not getting anything for this work. When the school started to return the checks, then the government agency started to send the checks directly to the families.

Guidelines for proper government grants management are found in Office of Management and Budget circulars. They can be found online at:
http://www.whitehouse.gov/omb/circulars/index.html

- OMB-A-110–*Uniform Administrative Requirements for Grants and Agreements with Institutions of Higher Education, Hospitals, and Other Non-profit Organizations*
- OMB-A-122-*Cost Principles of Non-Profit Organizations*
- OMB-A-133-*Audits of States, Local Governments, and Non-Profit Organizations*

Governmental grants have their own language, rules, and reporting requirements. They can be very complex. Some grants pay recipients based on head-counts during a period of time after service is provided. Some other grants pay ahead of time; some require reports to be provided before funds are released, etc.

Management of these grants can be challenging. Usually accounting departments are set up by grantors because each grant can be so different from another. Accounts payable and payroll can be centralized, but other processes are often separated by grant. Employees become specialized in dealing with specific accounting issues and reporting of certain grantors. In large organizations, contract departments are set up to deal with grant compliance and reporting.

*Organizations receiving government grants may set up summary worksheets on each grant contract with specific details on each one regarding requirements, reports, dates, etc. Instead of going through an entire contract to find an item, one could go to the summary.*

## Grant Management

The federal government has its own standards about managing grants, as reflected in the OMB Circular A-110,

*Uniform Administrative Requirements for Grants and Agreements with Institutions of Higher Education, Hospitals, and Other Non-Profit Organizations*, found at http://www.whitehouse.gov/omb/circulars/a110/a110.html

Non-profit organizations must have at minimum financial management systems that capture proper information for financial reports. The system must include adequate records reflecting the source and application of federal funds. In this area, computerized accounting and grant systems are valuable. Grants may run for a couple of years and then need to be closed. A non-profit cannot submit expenses for reimbursement on a grant that is closed, so timing is essential in a non-profit organization. Usually grants close a few months after it is over.

Non-profits should keep safe all documentation relating to authorizations, obligations, liabilities, assets, income, and interest.

Proper internal controls and written procedures should be available to safeguard assets. Actually, OMB Circular A-110 requires written procedures for cash management and for a cost allocation plan.

Expenses must be for authorized use only and a minimum time should lapse between funds received and spent. A proper documentation trail should be available for all expenses and reporting requirements should be complied with. Nowadays, online reports are the preferred method for reporting funds received and spent. If reports are not filed by a certain date, funds are not released by the government. Get all reporting deadlines in a calendar and don't forget them.

Most of the time, grants are booked as restricted funds because they are for a specific program and not for others. The challenge in this area for accounting is to be able to release funds through the "Net Assets Released from Restriction account." One cannot release net assets NOT spent. The release is limited by the amount of the grant. Suppose an organization has $100,000 in program expenses, but only an $80,000 balance for this grant. The release can be up to $80,000 and not $100,000. The difference is absorbed by the organization or the difference can be paid from another source. Make sure you understand that releasing funds doesn't mean that funds are available. Most of the time it means that expenses were used up, including overhead and that's why the funds were released.

Payments to non-profits are done as per grant contract. Many times organizations request a "drawdown" on a grant based on actual expenses plus the overhead rate, also known as the indirect rate, discussed later in this chapter. It is common for non-profits to draw down before payroll to help out with the cash outlay.

Depending on the grantor, payments can made monthly to the non-profit based on monthly expenses plus overhead. Usually government payments are off by a month. Billing sent out the beginning of January is usually paid in February. However, I have seen payments being very late because the non-profit is not providing the government with proper reports or is having other compliance issues.

Government typically pays drawdowns via wire transfers to a non-profit's bank accounts. If a large amount of funds is "parked" at the bank for days before being used, then the funds should earn interest. If the amount parked is material (more than $250 in interest or more than $120,000 in funding) then the interest should be applied as a credit or interest should be sent to the government.

Many government grants require matching funds. Volunteer work can be counted toward this "matching" along with donations of things -- in-kind contributions. So, a system must be in place to identify and account for both volunteer hours of professionals and donations of items to take advantage of this detail that can increase revenues.

Income generated by government-sponsored programs can be used in a few ways. Funds could be:

- Added to government funds already committed

- Used to finance the non-federal share of the project or program, in case of a matching situation

- Deducted from the total project or program allowable cost in determining the net allowable costs

It all depends on individual grant contracts.

OMB Circular A-110 describes property standards when funds are used to purchase equipment and real property. Key elements in this area are:

- o Inventory maintenance--Items need to be tagged and inventoried at least once every two years.

- o Procurement standards – The organization must have a written policy on code of conduct for personnel making buying decisions. The non-profit must adhere to standards of reasonableness, including consideration of minority/women-owned businesses, etc.

- o Specific language to be used on all non-profit's contracts with third parties, such as "Equal Employment Opportunity," "Anti-Kickback Act," and other compliance issues.

Government grants have budgets that are approved for the fiscal year. Sometimes more than a one-year budget is approved. Often budget numbers need to be revised. Sometimes errors happen in the original budget, unexpected things occur, or there is a major change in scope of services. Grant contracts may allow for changes, but each grant can be different.

Grant budget line items may have some flexibility. If a budget has five line items within the administrative section, then the total of administrative expenses is looked at and not really each line item. Sometimes prior approval is needed; sometimes it is not. If allowed, line item shifts are usually 10 percent of the total of each line item.

For instance, suppose a non-profit has an expense of $50 in postage-Administration that needs to be reimbursed by a grant. The postage line item in the budget has been spent. However, this organization has a line item for supplies that still has $500 left. The $50 would be approved for reimbursement even though its own line item is paid up. It all depends on the budget, the federal awarding agency, and the grant structure.

*Many state and local government grants refer to federal grants as the basis for their requirements. However, pay attention to local differences!!! For instance, the standard for capitalizing fixed assets per federal standards is $5,000. But the standard for capitalizing fixed assets per Los Angeles County is $500. Be mindful of odd discrepancies like that!*

OMB Circular A-110 has specific requirements for property disposition and other information. Make sure to keep at least one copy of this circular in the accounting office along with any changes or amendments.

Not all expenses can be charged to federal grants. The expense has to be somehow related to the project. OMB Circular A-122, *Cost Principles for Non-Profit Organizations,* provides guidelines in this area. OMB Circular A-122 is not for colleges and education institutions or hospitals or tribal governments. Other circulars cover these areas.

In order for costs to be allowed, they must be reasonable, consistent, documented, and must follow GAAP in accounting treatment. The government also keeps a list of companies that should NOT be used for funded projects. Firms in the list are not allowed and if a non-profit uses any of them, the cost will NOT be refunded. The website with more information on this topic can be found at www.epls.gov.

Organizations must use common sense and fairness in spending federal grants. Purchases of luxury items are usually not necessary and make no sense, especially when there are cheaper alternatives. Buying $200 wine bottles for the homeless, for instance, doesn't make any sense and is not a reasonable cost.

Costs may be funded by more than one grant and it is important to allocate costs properly to each funding source. Usually, one grant cannot cover for another grant deficiency, unless this is pre-approved.

To avoid misunderstandings, if certain items are odd, or if there are questions on the allowability and allocability of certain costs, they should be negotiated with the government in advance whenever possible. This is the same situation with consolidations and other exemptions; all need to be approved by a federal agency and the sooner, the better.

Be aware of specific educational requirements of personnel working on projects. I have seen an agency lose substantial funding because counselors in the program didn't have the minimum education requirements spelled out in the grant documentation. The loss happened after payroll expenses were incurred for the year and the agency had to absorb the loss. Tough lesson.

Pay attention to the definition of "fiscal year." Fiscal year per organization may be different as per grantor. This means that month 1 will be one for the grantor and another for internal accounting. Getting a project or grant module would be really helpful, since the reporting using the regular accounting system may be confusing. The grantor may require reports covering more than one accounting fiscal year. Grants could run from May to April or from October to September.

Different grants may also use a different allocation basis and items. While some grants may allow vacation pay to be included in indirect costs, others do not. The devil is in the details. Read all grant documentation carefully.

*Any organization that is basically funded with government grants should have a plan B to deal with government delays and other problems in funding. In California, for instance, many organizations stopped receiving funds because of budget problems. How do they survive? Many have lines of credit, negotiate major bills, etc... The point here is to have a plan B ready to go BEFORE you need it.*

Grant contracts involve many types of expenses/costs. They may include payroll, payroll taxes, supplies, rent, transportation, etc. Costs associated with grants can be summarized as:

- Direct costs
- *Plus* indirect costs
- *Less* credits on purchases and other expenses. These should be netted toward grant costs. For instance, if a non-profit receives a $100 rebate on a purchase using federal funding, the $100 should be netted against grant costs, decreasing them.

# Direct and Indirect costs

What are direct costs? Direct costs are those that can be easily identified with a program such as art supplies for an art program, art teachers who work only in that program, and mailing costs of the art program.

What are indirect costs? These are costs that are reasonable and allowed, but affect multiple programs and operations, not just in one area. Examples of indirect costs are depreciation in building and equipment, costs of operating and maintaining facilities, general administration and general expenses such as the accounting department, insurance, etc. Indirect costs are also known as "overhead."

Indirect costs can be classified within two broad categories:
1. "Facilities" includes depreciation and usage allowances on buildings, equipment, and capital improvement; operations and maintenance expenses; and interest on debt associated with buildings. Examples are janitorial expenses, security, and insurance related to the building.
2. "Administration" is defined as general administration and general expenses such as the executive's office, accounting, human resources, library expenses, and all other types of expenses not listed above.

Organizations receiving more than $10 million in direct costs must separate Facilities and Administration costs.

> *Be aware of differences between this type of classification and the standard cost accounting concepts. Mostly it is a new way to account for costs, but it is not GAAP per se. GAAP does not include "unallowed costs" and other concepts. This is an additional layer of complexity typical of non-profits.*

## Indirect Cost Management

Indirect costs can be a substantial part of grant expenses. Many times they are defined as a percentage to be applied towards direct expenses. I have seen rates as high as 88 percent of direct expenses.

OMB Circular A-122 provides guidance in this area. Non-profit organizations can have their own Cost Allocation Plans, where they derive indirect cost rates, or they can get official Indirect Cost Rates from the government. Sometimes they have both--one for one grant and the other for other grants. The idea is to have a reasonable way to charge indirect costs to different grants. One cannot charge costs to grants without basis.

# Cost Allocation Plans

Not all expenses are to be charged to grants. If a project has indirect expenses of $100,000, are all these costs going to be charged to grant A? Maybe. It depends. What if this project is funded by the grants? It all depends on the grant contract and cost allocation plans.

Cost allocation plans are methodologies used to allocate indirect costs to departments, grants, etc. These plans must be reasonable and consistent. A cost allocation plan can be submitted to certain government agencies to get a rate approved.

Often, after analysis, a rate is provided to non-profits by the government agency. Many times grants have different indirect cost rates. Some may have it at 15 percent, while others may have it at 60 percent, depending on the indirect and direct costs identified and the grant contract.

Direct costs are the base for indirect cost rate calculations. The main methodology is for the base to be the sum of direct costs charged to grants. Usually, the direct costs are direct salary costs or total direct costs.

The indirect and direct costs come from historical data. A rate is approved based on prior year expenses and applied toward this year expenses. This can create opportunities for planning for the following year. Many organizations want to classify as many direct costs to government grants as possible, so that the indirect cost rate for the following year is higher.

An indirect cost rate is a percentage calculated as:
Total Indirect Costs ($)/ Direct Cost base ($)
Example:
In year 2XX1 we have one grant and one project:

- Total Indirect Costs: $100,000
- Direct salaries and wages: $1,000,000 (Direct cost basis)

Indirect rate= 100,000/1,000,000=10%

Now we are in year 2XX2 and the 10% was approved.

If the grant has direct salaries and wages of $30,000 in year 2XX2:

Indirect Cost Recovery=$3,000 (10% of $30,000) can be charged

If the grant has direct salaries and wages of $20,000 in year 2XX2:

Indirect Cost Recovery=$2,000 (10% of $20,000) can be charged

On all indirect rate calculations, the basis (Direct Cost Basis) is very important. If the basis is "salaries and wages," then the rate should be applied to salaries and wages. If the basis is salaries and wages plus travel and utilities, then the rate should be applied accordingly the following year.

The basis can be made up of total direct costs (less capital expenses and other distorting items), direct salaries as wages (as per example), total costs, or another basis that makes sense. What works for one organization, may not work for another.

Most government grants do NOT cover fundraising costs.

Both direct and indirect costs exclude capital expenditures and unallowable costs. However, unallowable costs are included in the direct cost base (if they represent activities to which indirect costs are properly allocable).

In order to verify that the basis and calculations of indirect cost rates are reasonable, an analysis should be made comparing how much grant funding is received for indirect expenses and how much actual indirect expenses are. Depending on the difference, changes may be required to the rate or in the way the rate has been calculated. Indirect cost rates are usually not adjusted after approval. If the rate is not covering all the expenses, it may be too late and the organization may have to use other funds to cover the expenses.

The recognized ways to calculate and allocate indirect costs and rates per OMB Circular A-122 are:

> ➢ Simplified allocation
> ➢ Multiple allocation base
> ➢ Direct allocation
> ➢ Special indirect cost rates

The simplified allocation can be used when federal grants are not material, the organization has only one single function, and all programs benefit from indirect costs to about the same degree. The idea is to have one rate and go with it.

The multiple allocations method is used where an organization's indirect costs benefit its major functions in varying degrees. Indirect costs are accumulated in separate pools that hold similar characteristics and functions. Instead of getting one rate, the organization gets multiple rates.

Multiple allocations' pools of costs are classified as: 1) Depreciation and use allowance, 2) Interest, 3) Operations and maintenance expense, 4) Administration and general expenses. This is also the order in which the rates must be applied. (Many grantors also allow for payroll rates for taxes and benefits.)

The direct allocation method is used when an organization considers all expenses direct, except for General and Administration. The calculation and concept is the same as other methods for the indirect rate.

Sometimes organizations need special indirect cost rates to accommodate their individual needs. Those should be developed as other rates are calculated.

Many large organizations receiving substantial amounts of federal assistance get indirect cost rates pre-approved by a "cognizant" agency, usually the one funding the most dollars to the organization. This rate needs to be renewed yearly. This is known as the official "Indirect Cost Rate." Usually the non-profit must submit an allocation plan for approval every year.

Once this indirect cost rate is set, it can be applied to most federal grants. Also, many state and local grantors may accept this rate for their own grants.

The last OMB Circular to affect government grants is OMB Circular A-133. This is primarily for auditors, but gives all professionals good insights and guidance within the non-profit world. The government was spending too much time and money with separate audits and in 1984 the Single Audit Act was established. There have been some revisions, and currently OMB Circular A-133 provides audit standards for the Single Audit if a recipient spends $500,000 or more during the fiscal year. This amount may change over time. Note that the $500,000 is related to expenses, not grant revenues received.

Identification of federal funds can be tricky, since organizations my receive pass-through funds and may not know they are getting federal funds.

You can check the website http://www.whitehouse.gov/omb/rewrite/circulars/a133/a133.html for any changes in this area.

OMB Circular A-133 provides technical information for auditors (independent CPA firms) on grant compliance and other issues. The auditors' job in the Single Audit is to review and test internal controls and transactions to make sure grant funds were spent appropriately. The CPA firm releases a regular audit report plus extra ones regarding grant programs. A copy of the Single Audit report is forwarded to grantors.

Government grants can support many organizations, providing valuable services to the community. OMB Circulars 110, 122, and 133 provide some general accounting guidance in this area. Grant contracts can be complex, with indirect cost rates, allowable/unallowable costs, and other specific grant compliance issues. Once an organization starts getting federal funding, it may need to budget for a Single Audit in addition to the regular annual audit. Single Audit costs, if applicable, should be part of the grant contract and not be entirely funded by the non-profit.

# CHAPTER 7

## *FINANCIAL STATEMENTS*

*"I know at last what distinguishes man from animals: financial worries."*

Romain Rolland (French Writer, 1866-1944)

Non-profits may not have owners, but they have many interested parties. Bankers, board members, government entities, and donors are some of these interested parties who want to know how the organization is doing financially. Management and the board of directors usually get financial reports on a regular basis. These reports may or may not be based on GAAP, but they are important tools to manage organizations.

This chapter is about reporting according to GAAP. SFAS 117, *Financial Statements of Not-for-Profit Organizations*, provides guidance in this area. Some of the reports are quite similar to for-profit counterparts. You can read the full text at http://72.3.243.42/pdf/fas117.pdf

Next is a summary listing of financial reports. We will discuss each one of these financial statements in detail:

- The Statement of Financial Position is the non-profit's Balance Sheet

- The Statement of Activities is the non-profit's Income Statement
- The Statement of Cash Flows is a very similar report to the for–profit's Cash Flow Statement
- The Schedule of Functional Expenses is a unique non-profit report
- Other reports may be required for government grants recipients

*The Schedule of Functional Expenses ending balances should tie in with the Statement of Activities' expenses.*

*The Statement of Activities ending balances should tie in to the Statement of Financial Position.*

# The Statement of Financial Position

| Assets=Liability + Net Assets (Funds) |
| :---: |

This statement is similar to a regular balance sheet. The main difference is that instead of "Retained Earnings," this statement shows "Net Assets."

This statement should present information on all funds, unless it is detailed in notes to financial statements. This report is often shown with two years worth of information.

As with the balance sheet, the focus of the Statement of Financial Position is to show liquidity to all stakeholders. For instance, if a donor wants to donate $1 million to a charity, but sees $1,000 in cash, $2,000 in receivables, and over $500,000 in payables, this donor may think twice before donating.

Some interesting items of the Statement of Financial Position:

Cash and Cash Equivalents: These funds are on deposit in the bank or in very liquid and secure securities, such as U.S. Treasury bills. Be careful with the cash at year-end. I have seen an accountant who was too aggressive in moving funds from cash bank accounts to investments based on cash balances in the bank, forgetting about outstanding checks. The result was that this organization's cash account ended up with an odd negative balance at year end.

Pledges or Grants Receivable: These are commitments to donate and are shown at net realizable value--the value the organization expects to receive.

Prepaid expenses: These are amounts paid in advance that will decrease, as time passes. Usual examples are insurance and pre-paid rent.

Investments: These are stocks, bonds, and other investments at fair market value.

Fixed Assets or Property, Plant and Equipment: This line reflects the net book value of fixed assets--original cost less accumulated depreciation.

*Non-profit organizations used to expense all fixed assets and not capitalize them. After 1994, non-profits started to capitalize, as they were given the choice to capitalize old assets or not. So, many non-profits may have odd numbers for assets on the books, some capitalized and some not.*

Accounts Payable: This reflects the amounts owed to vendors. Unpaid salaries, taxes, or other large liabilities could be reported separately.

Grants Payable: These are promises made to individuals or other non-profits.

Refundable Advances: These are also known as "Deposits" or "Deferred Revenue." These are amounts (not donations) received that belong to another period. For example, this could be the fee of a course that is held the following fiscal year. Another example would be a donation received with a condition, not a restriction.

Long Term Debt: This includes principal and interest owed to creditors. This could be a bank loan, or bond or private debt financing.

Net Assets:

Unrestricted: These are net assets used for operations.

Temporarily restricted: These are net assets limited by donor-imposed stipulations that will expire with time or with another temporary limitation.

Permanently restricted: These are net assets limited by donor-imposed stipulations for life. For example, an endowment would be reported in this net asset.

The sequence of the items presented is based on liquidity, with the most liquid shown first. A Statement of Financial Position is used by banks to assess liquidity and ability to pay back loans.

*Summary version:*
Do Good Organization
Statement of Financial Position
12/31/20x0

Assets
|  |  |  |
|---|---|---|
| | Cash and cash equivalents | xxx |
| | Grant receivable-unrestricted | xxx |
| | Prepaid expenses | xxx |
| | Property and equipment | xxx |
| | Assets restricted- perm. Endowment | xxx |
| Total Assets | | xxx |

Liabilities
|  |  |  |
|---|---|---|
| | Accounts payable | xxx |
| | Deposits | xxx |
| Total Liabilities | | xxx |

Net Assets
|  |  |  |
|---|---|---|
| | Unrestricted | xxx |
| | Temporarily restricted | xxx |
| | Permanently restricted | xxx |
| Total Net Assets | | xxx |

Total Liabilities and Net Assets                                    xxx

*Classified statement version:*

Do good organization
Statement of Financial Position
June 30, 20X0

 Assets
 Current assets:

|  |  |
|---|---|
| Cash and cash equivalents | xxx |
| Short term investments | xxx |
| Grants receivable | xxx |
| Contributions receivable | |
| Unrestricted | xxx |
| Temporarily restricted | xxx |
| Total contribution receivable | xxx |
| | |
| Accounts receivable | xxx |
| Prepaid expenses | xxx |
| Total current assets | xxx |
| | |
| Property and equipment | xxx |
| Total Assets | xxx |
| | |
| Liabilities | |
| Current liabilities: | xxx |
| Accounts payable | xxx |
| Accrued expenses | xxx |
| Total current liabilities | xxx |
| | |
| Total liabilities | xxx |
| | |
| Net assets | |
| Unrestricted | xxx |
| Temporarily restricted | xxx |
| Permanently restricted | xxx |
| Total net assets | xxx |
| | |
| Total liabilities and net assets | xxx |

# The Statement of Activities

> **Revenues – Expenses= Change in Net Assets (funds) + Beginning Balance= Ending Net Asset Balance**

This is the statement where revenues and expenses are presented for a certain period of time. It is the "Income Statement" for non-profits. However, instead of showing a net income or loss at the bottom of the statement, it shows an "Increase in net assets" or a "Decrease in net assets." Then two lines follow: "Net assets at the beginning of year" and "Net assets at the end of the year."

A separate statement of changes in Net Assets can be prepared if there are unusual transactions within this area. This situation is atypical, but adjustments to Net Assets Balances can happen.

One of the major differences between the regular for-profit income statement and the non-profit version is that the non-profit statement shows information by fund/net asset type. A popular format is to show the statement of activities with columns for each fund type. Since mostly all expenses run through unrestricted funds, that's where most expenses should be shown.

Expenses are usually summarized by areas of Program, General/Administration, and Fundraising.

The Statement of Activities is also unique because it doesn't report profit or loss. The result of Revenues minus Expenses is the "Change in net assets."

Details of some other items showing up in this statement:

Contributions: Donations, contributions made by individuals or businesses, not government grants. (Grants are presented separately.)

Fundraising activities: Revenues originated from special events and campaigns.

Professional programs: Fees and other income received from programs.

Net Assets Released from Restriction: Temporarily restricted revenue/net assets used up in this period.

Net assets at the beginning of the year: Ending balance of the prior year brought forward.

Net assets at the end of the year: Beginning balance plus/minus changes in net assets. These numbers flow into the "Statement of Financial Position."

See the following example to illustrate the usages of this statement.

Do Good Organization

Statement of Activities

As of 6/30/0X

| REVENUE | Unrestricted | Temporarily Restricted | Permanently Restricted | Total |
|---|---|---|---|---|
| Contributions | 3,050 | 1,000 | 5,000 | 9,050 |
| Fundraising activities | 500 | 300 | | 800 |
| Professional programs | 100 | | | 100 |
| Net assets released | 300 | -300 | | - |
| TOTAL REVENUE | 3,950 | 1,000 | 5,000 | 9,950 |

| EXPENSES | | | | |
|---|---|---|---|---|
| Programs: | | | | |
| Program A | 350 | | | 350 |
| Program B | 220 | | | 220 |
| Program C | 150 | | | 150 |
| Management and general | 500 | | | 500 |
| Fundraising | 100 | | | 100 |
| TOTAL EXPENSES | 1,320 | - | - | 1,320 |
| Change in net assets | 2,630 | 1,000 | 5,000 | 8,630 |
| Net Assets at beg. of year | 2,500 | 500 | - | 3,000 |
| Net Assets at end of year | 5,130 | 1,500 | 5,000 | 11,630 |

# Statement of Cash Flows

> **Change in Cash = Cash from Operations + Cash from Investing + Cash from Financing**

This is very similar to the for-profit cash flow statement. The statement shows where cash came from and where it was used. The statement of cash flows assists donors and creditors in the following:

1. Ability to create positive cash flows in the future
2. Ability to pay program obligations and other financial obligations
3. Justification for differences between "Net assets increases/decreases" and cash receipts and payments
4. Details of cash and non-cash items, details of investments and other financial transactions

Per SFAS 117, the statement of cash flows is required as part of regular financial statements of a non-profit. Prior to SFAS 117, this statement was optional.

As with the for-profit cash flow statement, this one shows cash flows in three categories:

- Operating activities: All activities that are not investing or financing transactions, such as receiving general contributions, providing services, etc.
- Investing activities: Purchases and sales of investments.

- **Financing activities**: Transactions involving acquisition and repayment of capital, such as borrowings and payments. Purchases of property or equipment or any long-lived asset are shown in this section. This type of activity includes funds received that are restricted by donors for long-term use.

As in the for-profit world, Statement of Cash Flows can be prepared using the direct or the indirect methods.

Sample Statement of cash flows using the direct method:

Do-Good Charity
Statement of Cash Flows
For the Fiscal Year Ended June 30, 20X1

| | |
|---|---|
| Cash flows from operating activities: | |
| Cash received from service fees | xxx |
| Cash received from donors-contributors | xxx |
| Cash received from accounts receivable | xxx |
| Interest and dividends received | (xxx) |
| Interest paid | (xxx) |
| Cash paid to employees and vendors | (xxx) |
| Grants paid | (xxx) |
| Net cash provided by operating activities | xxx |
| | |
| Cash flows from investing activities: | |
| Purchase of land and building | (xxx) |
| Purchase of investments (stocks) | (xxx) |
| Proceeds from sales of investments | xxx |
| Purchases of investments | (xxx) |
| Net cash used by investing activities | xxx |

Cash flows from financing activities:

| | |
|---|---|
| Interest -restricted contrib- reinvestment | xxx |
| Payment of mortgage | (xxx) |
| Net cash used by financing activities | xxx |

| | |
|---|---|
| Net increase in cash and cash equivalents | xxx |
| Cash and cash equivalents at beginning of year | xxx |
| Cash and cash equivalents at end of year | xxx |

Reconciliation of change in net assets to net cash provided by oper. activities:

| | |
|---|---|
| Change in net assets | xxx |
| Adjustments to reconcile change in net assets to net cash | |
| by operating activities: | |
| Depreciation | xxx |
| Actuarial loss on annuity liability | xxx |
| Increase in accounts and interest receivable | (xxx) |
| Decrease in grants payable | (xxx) |
| Increase in accounts payable | xxx |
| Net cash provided by operating activities | xxx |

# Sample statement of cash flows using the indirect method:

Do-Good Charity
Statement of Cash Flows
For the Fiscal Year Ended June 30, 20X1

| | |
|---|---:|
| Cash flows from operating activities: | |
| Change in net assets | xxx |
| Adjustments to reconcile change in net assets to net cash used by operating Activities: | |
| Depreciation | xxx |
| Increase in accounts and interest receivable | (xxx) |
| Decrease in grants payable | (xxx) |
| Increase in accounts payable | xxx |
| Net cash provided by operating activities | xxx |
| | |
| Cash flows from investing activities: | |
| Purchase of equipment | (xxx) |
| Proceeds from sales of investments | xxx |
| Purchases of investments | (xxx) |
| Net cash used by investing activities | xxx |
| | |
| Cash flows from financing activities: | |
| Interest restricted- reinvestment | xxx |
| Payment of mortgage | (xxx) |
| Net cash used by financing activities | xxx |
| | |
| Net increase in cash and cash equivalents | xxx |
| Cash and cash equivalents at beginning of year | xxx |
| Cash and cash equivalents at end of year | xxx |

# Statement of Functional Expenses

| Total Expenses = Program Expenses + Fundraising Expenses + Administrative Expenses |
| --- |

This statement is typical of non-profit organizations with no real counterpart in the for-profit world. This statement is also known as the "Schedule of Functional Expenses." All expenses are allocated into Programs, General, and Administrative (G&A) and Fundraising in a matrix-like presentation. This statement presents details of expenses, such as payroll, rent, postage, etc.

Per SFAS 117, all voluntary health and welfare organizations must report functional expenses as well as natural classification. SFAS suggests, but doesn't require, other non-profits to provide expenses by natural classification.

The statement of functional expenses typically presents programs followed by G&A and then fundraising. An organization that has more than one program reports each program separately or groups them by nature or function. The natural categories are the lines of the statement, while the functional categories make up the columns.

Backups of the expense allocation methodology should be available. For instance, how was the "Personnel" line item calculated across the matrix? How was it allocated? These questions need to be answered with backup data.

Allocations are done based on reality, not on budget numbers. Timesheets and other evidence should "tie in" with the amounts allocated. Backups can be timesheets, including electronic ones, invoices, etc. These should clearly show that the expense was properly allocated.

An example of a Statement of Functional Expenses follows. The Programs area, shown as "Program Services," is spread into four columns because the organization has four different programs. Administration and Fundraising are shown as part of a "Supportive Service" umbrella. In the example, expenses seem to be up to par with other non-profits with the programs area presenting the most expenses, followed by Administration and Fundraising.

*Statement of Functional Expenses- Part IX on the 990 is classified by the same three areas. Line items may be different than the ones in the financial statement. Look out for the joint costs checkbox at the bottom of the form. (Joint costs are discussed next.)*

| | Program Services | | | | Supporting Services | | |
|---|---|---|---|---|---|---|---|
| Do-very-well-organization | | | | | | | |
| Statement of Functional Expenses | | | | | | | |
| 6/30/20XX | | | | | | | |
| | Animal Advocacy | Public Education | Primate Sanctuary | Bird Program | Administr. | Fundraising | Total |
| Personnel | $546,999 | $112,333 | $98,746 | $18,746 | $155,236 | $58,999 | $991,059 |
| Consultants | 62,333 | 57,949 | | | 19,972 | 27,881 | $168,135 |
| Legal and accounting | 15,866 | | 3,368 | 1,699 | 35,229 | | $56,162 |
| Postage and delivery | 10,496 | 99,687 | 235 | | 10,103 | 12,587 | $133,108 |
| Print/publications | 2,630 | 58,666 | | | 8,327 | 2,396 | $72,019 |
| Feed | | | 128,991 | | | | $128,991 |
| Depreciation | 8,991 | 2,580 | 3,669 | 1588 | 8,999 | 877 | $26,704 |
| Contributions | 6,333 | | | | | | $6,333 |
| Advertising /Promotion | 47,777 | 26,888 | | | 2,041 | 11,982 | $88,688 |
| Investment expenses | 10,001 | 8,613 | 7,863 | | 5,284 | 3,954 | $35,715 |
| Travel and conferences | 20,336 | 2,553 | 2,995 | 1,036 | 1,702 | 95 | $28,717 |
| Telecommunications | 11,764 | 4,246 | 5,804 | | 1,868 | 679 | $24,361 |
| Utilities | 5,688 | 2,781 | 9,984 | | 3,660 | 967 | $23,080 |
| Insurance | 4,271 | 1,280 | 13,017 | | 2,204 | 1355 | $22,127 |
| Equipment maintenance | 1,039 | 742 | 3,373 | | 686 | 371 | $6,211 |
| Veterinary | 8,941 | | 2,445 | 778 | | | $12,164 |
| Fac. Maint. | | | 2,719 | | | | $2,719 |
| Other | 6,999 | 2,333 | 875 | | 566 | 2,699 | $13,472 |
| Total | $770,464 | $380,651 | $284,084 | $23,847 | $255,877 | $124,842 | $1,839,765 |

As is the case with many non-profits, the salaries line shows the most expenses. Accordingly, attention should be given to this area to make sure it is reasonable. Many times employees move around, working in different areas, but the payroll coding in the system remains the same. Changes to payroll coding and timesheets should be reviewed often. Consultants are the second biggest expense and consulting for fundraising should be investigated. Were they paid based on commission? (This is a big no-no).

## Joint Costs

One of the challenges of allocating expenses is the issue of joint cost. This is really not about overhead allocation/indirect costs allocation as discussed in the government grant chapter. The term "joint costs" is about fundraising expenses. These are expenses that belong to fundraising and at least one more area.

For example, a brochure could have elements of both fundraising and programs. This is an important topic because traditionally non-profits prefer to allocate the most to programs and the least to fundraising. Why? Because usually donors favor non-profits that spend the most in programs and the least in fundraising. Until 1998, this issue was problematic with no clear methodology to follow and no real consistency.

In 1998, this problem was addressed by the AICPA Statement of Position 98-2, *"Accounting for Costs of Activities of Not-for-Profit Organizations and State and Local Governmental Entities."* This SOP gives a three criteria frame of reference and requires that allocations be rational and systematic.

The idea is to set up rules/criteria so that joint costs could be allocated to program and G&A in a consistent matter. The criteria are related to:

1. Purpose of the event
2. Audience
3. Content

Criteria must be applied in this specific order.
www.aicpa.org

Specific questions are asked to determine whether costs should be completely allocated to fundraising, or not. Make sure to read up on this SOP and to have it handy.

Interestingly, the standard doesn't specify the method for allocating costs other than that the method should be rational and systematic. All joint costs are reported in the Statement of Functional Expenses in detail after allocation is done.

Non-profits' financial statements are to be used by all stakeholders, including bankers, to assess liquidity and the financial health of the organization. Allocating expenses between fundraising and other areas is important to report expenses in financial statements fairly. Statement of Position functions like the Balance Sheet of the non-profit. Statement of Activities functions like the Income Statement; and the Cash Flow Statement has the same purpose as the

Cash Flow Statement in the for-profit area. These statements are the minimum required by SFAS 117.

# CHAPTER 8

## *TAXATION*

*"The hardest thing to understand in the world is the income tax."*
Albert Einstein

It can be a surprise to know that non-profit organizations file tax returns. Many times it is just an information return, but other times, non-profits pay federal or state or even local taxes. This chapter will be mostly about federal reporting requirements.

Non-profits are generally required to file one or more of these tax returns annually due on the 15th day of the 5th month after closing of the year:

- 990: *Return of Organization Exempt from Income Tax*
- 990-EZ: *Short Form Return of Organization Exempt from Income Tax*
- 990-N*: e-Postcard*
- 990-T: *Exempt Organization Business Income Tax Return*

The newest form is the 990-N. It is a simple electronic form to be filed by organizations with regular gross receipts of $25,000 or less in 2008 and 2009; and gross receipts less than $50,000 for 2010.

Per the IRS website:

An organization's gross receipts are considered to be $25,000 or less if the organization:

- Has been in existence for one year or less and received, or donors have pledged to give, $37,500 or less during the organization's first tax year
- Has been in existence between one and three years and averaged $30,000 or less in gross receipts during each of its first two tax years, or
- Is at least three years old and averaged $25,000 or less in gross receipts for the immediately preceding three tax years (including the year for which calculations are being made) http://www.irs.gov/charities/article/0,,id=177338,00.html if this link doesn't work, try www.irs.gov

990-N asks for identification information on the non-profit and a confirmation of the organization's annual gross receipts.

There is no penalty for failing to file the 990-N form; however, organizations not filing for three years in a row will have their tax-exempt status revoked. The organization will need to file new exemption forms and fees.

Annual information reports such as 990 and 990-EZ are required to be filed by larger organizations. If not filed for three consecutive years, the organization may lose its tax exempt status and may need to re-apply.

Per the IRS, the following applies:

The new Form 990 series returns will be effective for 2008 tax years (returns filed beginning in 2009). To allow organizations time to adjust to the new forms, the IRS is phasing in the new returns during a three-year transition period. During the transition, an organization's annual filing requirement will depend on its financial activity. The charts next present annual exempt organization filing requirements during the transition period.

For all years, sponsoring organizations of donor advised funds and controlling organizations described in section 512(b)(13) must file Form 990 regardless of the amount of their gross receipts or assets.

http://www.irs.gov/charities/article/0,,id=184445,00.html
If the link doesn't work, try www.irs.gov

| 2007 Tax Year (Filed in 2008 or 2009) | Form to File |
|---|---|
| Gross receipts normally ≤ $25,000 | 990-N |
| Gross receipts > $25,000 and < $100,000, and Total assets < $250,000 | 990-EZ or 990 |
| Gross receipts ≥ $100,000, or Total assets ≥ $250,000 | 990 |

| 2008 Tax Year<br>(Filed in 2009 or 2010) | Form to File |
|---|---|
| Gross receipts normally ≤ $25,000 | 990-N |
| Gross receipts > $25,000 and < $ 1 million, and Total assets < $2.5 million | 990-EZ or 990 |
| Gross receipts ≥ $1 million, or Total assets ≥ $2.5 million | 990 |

| 2009 Tax Year<br>(Filed in 2010 or 2011) | Form to File |
|---|---|
| Gross receipts normally ≤ $25,000 | 990-N |
| Gross receipts > $25,000 and < $500,000, and Total assets < $1.25 million | 990-EZ or 990 |
| Gross receipts ≥ $500,000, or Total assets ≥ $1.25 million | 990 |

| 2010 Tax Year and later<br>(Filed in 2011 and later) | Form to File |
|---|---|
| Gross receipts normally ≤$50,000 | 990-N |
| Gross receipts > $50,000 and < $200,000, and Total assets < $500,000 | 990-EZ or 990 |
| Gross receipts ≥ $200,000, or Total assets ≥ $500,000 | 990 |

Non-profit organizations are required to pay taxes in their Unrelated Business Taxable Income (UBTI), even if they only have to file the 990-N form.

If an organization has UBTI of $1,000, it must file 990-T. Unrelated Business Taxable Income is defined as income not substantially related to the organization's tax exempt purposes or activities. This tax was set up so that not-profit organizations do not compete unfairly with for-profit entities. This area is under extra scrutiny by the IRS lately.

Generally, an activity generates unrelated business income if it meets three requirements:

1. It is a trade or business
2. It is regularly carried on, and
3. It is not substantially related to furthering the exempt purpose of the organization

For example, a non-profit organization runs a pizza parlor selling pizza to the public. The non-profit mission and programs have nothing to do with the parlor. The non-profit pays employees to run the pizza place. The pizza parlor generates unrelated business income.

On the other hand, a humanitarian-service non-profit holds a bake sale. While the sale is unrelated to the mission, it may be tax exempt if it is not regularly carried on. Business activities of an organization usually are considered regularly carried on if they show a frequency and continuity, and are pursued in a manner similar to comparable commercial activities of for-profit businesses. If a non-profit is not competing with a for-profit business, most likely it is not generating UBTI.

There are other types of unrelated business activities that are not taxed as UBTI. For instance, if the goods that the organization sells were donated or substantially all of the labor involved in the business is performed by volunteers, then there is no unrelated business income. Volunteer labor is often the key component to avoid UBTI situations.

## Form 990

The IRS has revised the form 990 and others related to non-profit organizations. Some of the changes from the old 990 to new 990 are:

--Revenues and expenses are required for two years, not just one, as in the old 990

--The mission statement is required on the new 990. This is mostly because some unscrupulous organizations get the 501c (3) certification and then change programs radically.

--There are new questions about governance, including board reviews of 990 before it is filed.

--The new form contains eleven core pages and sixteen schedules.

For more specific information on changes, please visit: http://www.irs.gov/charities/article/0,,id=188585,00.html

Current law requires that non-profits make their tax returns available to anyone who asks. So, many returns are posted on their websites or in data banks, such as www.guidestar.org.

Be aware that part of the 990 includes salary information for highly paid executives and consultants. This is not confidential information. There are also questions about contractors and consultants, donors, etc. that will not be kept confidential because it is part of the 990.

> *990 requests specific questions about compliance with payroll taxes, contractors' filings, and even a question about W-2-G for game/raffle winnings.*

Many organizations use 990s as marketing tools to showcase their programs and accomplishments. It is not unusual to have extensive attachments to 990 to show details of programs and the good they do in the community.

Numbers in the 990 must match or be reconciled with book numbers. Make sure all reconciling items are known and available for review.

Often, auditors prepare the 990, as they prepare financial statements. Organizations attach detailed information on programs and specific accomplishments toward the back of the return as a marketing tool.

Non-profit organizations can file for extensions to file information/tax returns. Next is a sample of some pages of the 990:

Form **990**

## Return of Organization Exempt From Income Tax

Under section 501(c), 527, or 4947(a)(1) of the Internal Revenue Code (except black lung benefit trust or private foundation)

The organization may have to use a copy of this return to satisfy state reporting requirements.

Department of the Treasury
Internal Revenue Service

**2008**

**Open to Public Inspection**

**A**  For the 2008 calendar year, or tax year beginning _____ , 2008, and ending _____ , 20 ___

| **B** Check if applicable: | Please use IRS label or print or type. See Specific Instruc- tions. | **C** Name of organization | | | **D** Employer identification number |
|---|---|---|---|---|---|
| ☐ Address change | | Doing Business As | | | |
| ☐ Name change | | Number and street (or P.O. box if mail is not delivered to street address) | Room/suite | | **E** Telephone number ( ) |
| ☐ Initial return | | City or town, state or country, and ZIP + 4 | | | |
| ☐ Termination | | | | | **G** Gross receipts $ |
| ☐ Amended return | | | | | |
| ☐ Application pending | **F** Name and address of principal officer: | | | **H(a)** Is this a group return for affiliates? ☐ Yes ☐ No | |
| | | | | **H(b)** Are all affiliates included? ☐ Yes ☐ No If "No," attach a list. (see instructions) | |

**I**  Tax-exempt status:  ☐ 501(c) ( ) ◄ (insert no.)  ☐ 4947(a)(1) or  ☐ 527

**J**  Website: ►

**H(c)** Group exemption number ►

**K**  Type of organization: ☐ Corporation ☐ Trust ☐ Association ☐ Other ►  **L** Year of formation:  **M** State of legal domicile:

### Part I  Summary

| | | | |
|---|---|---|---|
| **Activities & Governance** | 1 | Briefly describe the organization's mission or most significant activities: _____ | |
| | 2 | Check this box ► ☐ if the organization discontinued its operations or disposed of more than 25% of its assets. | |
| | 3 | Number of voting members of the governing body (Part VI, line 1a) .......................... | **3** |
| | 4 | Number of independent voting members of the governing body (Part VI, line 1b) .......... | **4** |
| | 5 | Total number of employees (Part V, line 2a)................................................. | **5** |
| | 6 | Total number of volunteers (estimate if necessary) ...................................... | **6** |
| | 7a | Total gross unrelated business revenue from Part VIII, column (C).................... | **7a** |
| | b | Net unrelated business taxable income from Form 990-T, line 34 ............................ | **7b** |

| | | | Prior Year | Current Year |
|---|---|---|---|---|
| **Revenue** | 8 | Contributions and grants (Part VIII, line 1h) .................................... | | |
| | 9 | Program service revenue (Part VIII, line 2g).................................... | | |
| | 10 | Investment income (Part VIII, column (A), lines 3, 4, and 7d) ................. | | |
| | 11 | Other revenue (Part VIII, column (A), lines 5, 6d, 8c, 9c, 10c, and 11e) .... | | |
| | 12 | Total revenue—add lines 8 through 11 (must equal Part VIII, column (A), line 12 ) | | |
| **Expenses** | 13 | Grants and similar amounts paid (Part IX, column (A), lines 1–3)............. | | |
| | 14 | Benefits paid to or for members (Part IX, column (A), line 4) ................. | | |
| | 15 | Salaries, other compensation, employee benefits (Part IX, column (A), lines 5–10) | | |
| | 16a | Professional fundraising fees (Part IX, column (A), line 11e) ................. | | |
| | b | Total fundraising expenses (Part IX, column (D), line 25) ► | | |
| | 17 | Other expenses (Part IX, column (A), lines 11a–11d, 11f–24f)................. | | |
| | 18 | Total expenses. Add lines 13–17 (must equal Part IX, column (A), line 25)... | | |
| | 19 | Revenue less expenses. Subtract line 18 from line 12 ........................ | | |

| | | | Beginning of Year | End of Year |
|---|---|---|---|---|
| **Net Assets or Fund Balances** | 20 | Total assets (Part X, line 16).................................................... | | |
| | 21 | Total liabilities (Part X, line 26) ................................................ | | |
| | 22 | Net assets or fund balances. Subtract line 21 from line 20 .................... | | |

### Part II  Signature Block

Under penalties of perjury, I declare that I have examined this return, including accompanying schedules and statements, and to the best of my knowledge and belief, it is true, correct, and complete. Declaration of preparer (other than officer) is based on all information of which preparer has any knowledge.

| **Sign Here** | | | |
|---|---|---|---|
| | Signature of officer | | Date |
| | Type or print name and title | | |

| **Paid Preparer's Use Only** | Preparer's signature | | Date | Check if self-employed ☐ | Preparer's identifying number (see instructions) |
|---|---|---|---|---|---|
| | Firm's name (or yours if self-employed), address, and ZIP + 4 | | | EIN | |
| | | | | Phone no. ( ) | |

May the IRS discuss this return with the preparer shown above? (see instructions)  ..........................  ☐ Yes ☐ No

**For Privacy Act and Paperwork Reduction Act Notice, see the separate instructions.**  Cat. No. 11282Y  Form **990** (2008)

| Part III | Statement of Program Service Accomplishments (see instructions) |
|---|---|

1   Briefly describe the organization's mission:

_____

_____

_____

2   Did the organization undertake any significant program services during the year which were not listed on
    the prior Form 990 or 990-EZ? ..........................................................................................   ☐ Yes ☐ No
    If "Yes," describe these new services on Schedule O.

3   Did the organization cease conducting, or make significant changes in how it conducts, any program
    services? ...............................................................................................................   ☐ Yes ☐ No
    If "Yes," describe these changes on Schedule O.

4   Describe the exempt purpose achievements for each of the organization's three largest program services by expenses.
    Section 501(c)(3) and 501(c)(4) organizations and section 4947(a)(1) trusts are required to report the amount of grants and
    allocations to others, the total expenses, and revenue, if any, for each program service reported.

4a  (Code: _____ ) (Expenses $ _____ including grants of $ _____ ) (Revenue $ _____ )

_____

_____

_____

_____

_____

_____

_____

_____

4b  (Code: _____ ) (Expenses $ _____ including grants of $ _____ ) (Revenue $ _____ )

_____

_____

_____

_____

_____

_____

_____

_____

4c  (Code: _____ ) (Expenses $ _____ including grants of $ _____ ) (Revenue $ _____ )

_____

_____

_____

_____

_____

_____

_____

4d  Other program services. (Describe in Schedule O.)
    (Expenses $ _____ including grants of $ _____ ) (Revenue $ _____ )

4e  **Total program service expenses**  $ _____   *(Must equal Part IX, Line 25, column (B).)*

Form **990** (2008)

142

| Part IV | Checklist of Required Schedules | | |
|---|---|---|---|

| | | Yes | No |
|---|---|---|---|
| **1** | Is the organization described in section 501(c)(3) or 4947(a)(1) (other than a private foundation)? *If "Yes," complete Schedule A* ..................................................................................... **1** | | |
| **2** | Is the organization required to complete Schedule B, Schedule of Contributors? ........................... **2** | | |
| **3** | Did the organization engage in direct or indirect political campaign activities on behalf of or in opposition to candidates for public office? *If "Yes," complete Schedule C, Part I* ......................................... **3** | | |
| **4** | **Section 501(c)(3) organizations.** Did the organization engage in lobbying activities? *If "Yes," complete Schedule C, Part II* ............................................................................................. **4** | | |
| **5** | **Section 501(c)(4), 501(c)(5), and 501(c)(6) organizations.** Is the organization subject to the section 6033(e) notice and reporting requirement and proxy tax? *If "Yes," complete Schedule C, Part III* ................... **5** | | |
| **6** | Did the organization maintain any donor advised funds or any accounts where donors have the right to provide advice on the distribution or investment of amounts in such funds or accounts? *If "Yes," complete Schedule D, Part I* .......................................................................................... **6** | | |
| **7** | Did the organization receive or hold a conservation easement, including easements to preserve open space, the environment, historic land areas, or historic structures? *If "Yes," complete Schedule D, Part II* ...... **7** | | |
| **8** | Did the organization maintain collections of works of art, historical treasures, or other similar assets? *If "Yes," complete Schedule D, Part III* .............................................................................. **8** | | |
| **9** | Did the organization report an amount in Part X, line 21; serve as a custodian for amounts not listed in Part X; or provide credit counseling, debt management, credit repair, or debt negotiation services? *If "Yes," complete Schedule D, Part IV* ..................................................................................... **9** | | |
| **10** | Did the organization hold assets in term, permanent, or quasi-endowments? *If "Yes," complete Schedule D, Part V* **10** | | |
| **11** | Did the organization report an amount in Part X, lines 10, 12, 13, 15, or 25? *If "Yes," complete Schedule D, Parts VI, VII, VIII, IX, or X as applicable* ............................................................ **11** | | |
| **12** | Did the organization receive an audited financial statement for the year for which it is completing this return that was prepared in accordance with GAAP? *If "Yes," complete Schedule D, Parts XI, XII, and XIII* ....... **12** | | |
| **13** | Is the organization a school described in section 170(b)(1)(A)(ii)? *If "Yes," complete Schedule E* ............... **13** | | |
| **14a** | Did the organization maintain an office, employees, or agents outside of the U.S.? ......................... **14a** | | |
| **b** | Did the organization have aggregate revenues or expenses of more than $10,000 from grantmaking, fundraising, business, and program service activities outside the U.S.? *If "Yes," complete Schedule F, Part I* ............... **14b** | | |
| **15** | Did the organization report on Part IX, column (A), line 3, more than $5,000 of grants or assistance to any organization or entity located outside the United States? *If "Yes," complete Schedule F, Part II* ............ **15** | | |
| **16** | Did the organization report on Part IX, column (A), line 3, more than $5,000 of aggregate grants or assistance to individuals located outside the United States? *If "Yes," complete Schedule F, Part III* ................... **16** | | |
| **17** | Did the organization report more than $15,000 on Part IX, column (A), line 11e? *If "Yes," complete Schedule G, Part I* **17** | | |
| **18** | Did the organization report more than $15,000 total on Part VIII, lines 1c and 8a? *If "Yes," complete Schedule G, Part II* **18** | | |
| **19** | Did the organization report more than $15,000 on Part VIII, line 9a? *If "Yes," complete Schedule G, Part III* **19** | | |
| **20** | Did the organization operate one or more hospitals? *If "Yes," complete Schedule H* ..................... **20** | | |
| **21** | Did the organization report more than $5,000 on Part IX, column (A), line 1? *If "Yes," complete Schedule I, Parts I and II* **21** | | |
| **22** | Did the organization report more than $5,000 on Part IX, column (A), line 2? *If "Yes," complete Schedule I, Parts I and III* **22** | | |
| **23** | Did the organization answer "Yes" to Part VII, Section A, questions 3, 4, or 5? *If "Yes," complete Schedule J* ................................................................................................ **23** | | |
| **24a** | Did the organization have a tax-exempt bond issue with an outstanding principal amount of more than $100,000 as of the last day of the year, that was issued after December 31, 2002? *If "Yes," answer questions 24b–24d and complete Schedule K. If "No," go to question 25* ............................................... **24a** | | |
| **b** | Did the organization invest any proceeds of tax-exempt bonds beyond a temporary period exception? .... **24b** | | |
| **c** | Did the organization maintain an escrow account other than a refunding escrow at any time during the year to defease any tax-exempt bonds? ...................................................................... **24c** | | |
| **d** | Did the organization act as an "on behalf of" issuer for bonds outstanding at any time during the year? **24d** | | |
| **25a** | **Section 501(c)(3) and 501(c)(4) organizations.** Did the organization engage in an excess benefit transaction with a disqualified person during the year? *If "Yes," complete Schedule L, Part I* .......................... **25a** | | |
| **b** | Did the organization become aware that it had engaged in an excess benefit transaction with a disqualified person from a prior year? *If "Yes," complete Schedule L, Part I* .............................................. **25b** | | |
| **26** | Was a loan to or by a current or former officer, director, trustee, key employee, highly compensated employee, or disqualified person outstanding as of the end of the organization's tax year? *If "Yes," complete Schedule L, Part II* .... **26** | | |
| **27** | Did the organization provide a grant or other assistance to an officer, director, trustee, key employee, or substantial contributor, or to a person related to such an individual? *If "Yes," complete Schedule L, Part III* **27** | | |

Form **990** (2008)

| Part IV | Checklist of Required Schedules *(continued)* |

|  |  | Yes | No |
|---|---|---|---|

**28** During the tax year, did any person who is a current or former officer, director, trustee, or key employee:

**a** Have a direct business relationship with the organization (other than as an officer, director, trustee, or employee), or an indirect business relationship through ownership of more than 35% in another entity (individually or collectively with other person(s) listed in Part VII, Section A)? *If "Yes," complete Schedule L, Part IV* ............................................................................................................ **28a**

**b** Have a family member who had a direct or indirect business relationship with the organization? *If "Yes," complete Schedule L, Part IV* ............................................................................................... **28b**

**c** Serve as an officer, director, trustee, key employee, partner, or member of an entity (or a shareholder of a professional corporation) doing business with the organization? *If "Yes," complete Schedule L, Part IV* .... **28c**

**29** Did the organization receive more than $25,000 in non-cash contributions? *If "Yes," complete Schedule M* **29**

**30** Did the organization receive contributions of art, historical treasures, or other similar assets, or qualified conservation contributions? *If "Yes," complete Schedule M* ............................................................. **30**

**31** Did the organization liquidate, terminate, or dissolve and cease operations? *If "Yes," complete Schedule N, Part I* .................................................................................................................................. **31**

**32** Did the organization sell, exchange, dispose of, or transfer more than 25% of its net assets? *If "Yes," complete Schedule N, Part II* ............................................................................................................. **32**

**33** Did the organization own 100% of an entity disregarded as separate from the organization under Regulations sections 301.7701-2 and 301.7701-3? *If "Yes," complete Schedule R, Part I* .................................... **33**

**34** Was the organization related to any tax-exempt or taxable entity? *If "Yes," complete Schedule R, Parts II, III, IV, and V, line 1* ............................................................................................................... **34**

**35** Is any related organization a controlled entity within the meaning of section 512(b)(13)? *If "Yes," complete Schedule R, Part V, line 2* ........................................................................................................ **35**

**36** **Section 501(c)(3) organizations.** Did the organization make any transfers to an exempt non-charitable related organization? *If "Yes," complete Schedule R, Part V, line 2* ........................................................... **36**

**37** Did the organization conduct more than 5% of its activities through an entity that is not a related organization and that is treated as a partnership for federal income tax purposes? *If "Yes," complete Schedule R, Part VI* ....................................................................................................................................... **37**

## Part V　Statements Regarding Other IRS Filings and Tax Compliance

|  |  | Yes | No |
|---|---|---|---|

**1a** Enter the number reported in Box 3 of Form 1096, Annual Summary and Transmittal of U.S. Information Returns. Enter -0- if not applicable ................................. `1a`

**b** Enter the number of Forms W-2G included in line 1a. Enter -0- if not applicable .... `1b`

**c** Did the organization comply with backup withholding rules for reportable payments to vendors and reportable gaming (gambling) winnings to prize winners? ........................................................... **1c**

**2a** Enter the number of employees reported on Form W-3, Transmittal of Wage and Tax Statements, filed for the calendar year ending with or within the year covered by this return `2a`

**b** If at least one is reported on line 2a, did the organization file all required federal employment tax returns? **2b**

**Note.** If the sum of lines 1a and 2a is greater than 250, you may be required to e-*file* this return. (see instructions)

**3a** Did the organization have unrelated business gross income of $1,000 or more during the year covered by this return? ................................................................................ **3a**

**b** If "Yes," has it filed a Form 990-T for this year? If *"No," provide an explanation in Schedule O* .......... **3b**

**4a** At any time during the calendar year, did the organization have an interest in, or a signature or other authority over, a financial account in a foreign country (such as a bank account, securities account, or other financial account)? ................................................................................................. **4a**

**b** If "Yes," enter the name of the foreign country: _____

See the instructions for exceptions and filing requirements for Form TD F 90-22.1, Report of Foreign Bank and Financial Accounts.

**5a** Was the organization a party to a prohibited tax shelter transaction at any time during the tax year? ....... **5a**

**b** Did any taxable party notify the organization that it was or is a party to a prohibited tax shelter transaction? **5b**

**c** If "Yes," to question 5a or 5b, did the organization file Form 8886-T, Disclosure by Tax-Exempt Entity Regarding Prohibited Tax Shelter Transaction? ................................................... **5c**

**6a** Did the organization solicit any contributions that were not tax deductible? ............................ **6a**

**b** If "Yes," did the organization include with every solicitation an express statement that such contributions or gifts were not tax deductible? ......................................................................... **6b**

**7** **Organizations that may receive deductible contributions under section 170(c).**

**a** Did the organization provide goods or services in exchange for any quid pro quo contribution of more than $75? ................................................................................................. **7a**

**b** If "Yes," did the organization notify the donor of the value of the goods or services provided? .......... **7b**

**c** Did the organization sell, exchange, or otherwise dispose of tangible personal property for which it was required to file Form 8282? ................................................................. **7c**

**d** If "Yes," indicate the number of Forms 8282 filed during the year .................... `7d`

**e** Did the organization, during the year, receive any funds, directly or indirectly, to pay premiums on a personal benefit contract? ................................................................................. **7e**

**f** Did the organization, during the year, pay premiums, directly or indirectly, on a personal benefit contract? **7f**

**g** For all contributions of qualified intellectual property, did the organization file Form 8899 as required? . **7g**

**h** For contributions of cars, boats, airplanes, and other vehicles, did the organization file a Form 1098-C as required? ................................................................................................. **7h**

**8** **Section 501(c)(3) and other sponsoring organizations maintaining donor advised funds and section 509(a)(3) supporting organizations.** Did the supporting organization, or a fund maintained by a sponsoring organization, have excess business holdings at any time during the year? ............................... **8**

**9** **Section 501(c)(3) and other sponsoring organizations maintaining donor advised funds.**

**a** Did the organization make any taxable distributions under section 4966? ............................. **9a**

**b** Did the organization make a distribution to a donor, donor advisor, or related person? ................... **9b**

**10** **Section 501(c)(7) organizations.** Enter:

**a** Initiation fees and capital contributions included on Part VIII, line 12 ................... `10a`

**b** Gross receipts, included on Form 990, Part VIII, line 12, for public use of club facilities `10b`

**11** **Section 501(c)(12) organizations.** Enter:

**a** Gross income from members or shareholders ........................................... `11a`

**b** Gross income from other sources (Do not net amounts due or paid to other sources against amounts due or received from them.) ............................................................. `11b`

**12a** **Section 4947(a)(1) non-exempt charitable trusts.** Is the organization filing Form 990 in lieu of Form 1041? **12a**

**b** If "Yes," enter the amount of tax-exempt interest received or accrued during the year . `12b`

Form **990** (2008)

145

**Part VI** Governance, Management, and Disclosure *(Sections A, B, and C request information about policies not required by the Internal Revenue Code.)*

### Section A. Governing Body and Management

|  | | Yes | No |
|---|---|---|---|
| *For each "Yes" response to lines 2–7b below, and for a "No" response to lines 8 or 9b below, describe the circumstances, processes, or changes in Schedule O. See instructions.* | | | |
| **1a** Enter the number of voting members of the governing body ........................ **1a** | | | |
| **b** Enter the number of voting members that are independent ......................... **1b** | | | |
| **2** Did any officer, director, trustee, or key employee have a family relationship or a business relationship with any other officer, director, trustee, or key employee? ...................................... | **2** | | |
| **3** Did the organization delegate control over management duties customarily performed by or under the direct supervision of officers, directors or trustees, or key employees to a management company or other person? . | **3** | | |
| **4** Did the organization make any significant changes to its organizational documents since the prior Form 990 was filed? | **4** | | |
| **5** Did the organization become aware during the year of a material diversion of the organization's assets? | **5** | | |
| **6** Does the organization have members or stockholders? ............................................. | **6** | | |
| **7a** Does the organization have members, stockholders, or other persons who may elect one or more members of the governing body? | **7a** | | |
| **b** Are any decisions of the governing body subject to approval by members, stockholders, or other persons? .... | **7b** | | |
| **8** Did the organization contemporaneously document the meetings held or written actions undertaken during the year by the following: | | | |
| **a** The governing body? ............................................................................ | **8a** | | |
| **b** Each committee with authority to act on behalf of the governing body? ............................. | **8b** | | |
| **9a** Does the organization have local chapters, branches, or affiliates? ................................. | **9a** | | |
| **b** If "Yes," does the organization have written policies and procedures governing the activities of such chapters, affiliates, and branches to ensure their operations are consistent with those of the organization? ............. | **9b** | | |
| **10** Was a copy of the Form 990 provided to the organization's governing body before it was filed? All organizations must describe in Schedule O the process, if any, the organization uses to review the Form 990 ............... | **10** | | |
| **11** Is there any officer, director or trustee, or key employee listed in Part VII, Section A, who cannot be reached at the organization's mailing address? *If "Yes," provide the names and addresses in Schedule O* ................. | **11** | | |

### Section B. Policies

|  | | Yes | No |
|---|---|---|---|
| **12a** Does the organization have a written conflict of interest policy? *If "No," go to line 13* .................... | **12a** | | |
| **b** Are officers, directors or trustees, and key employees required to disclose annually interests that could give rise to conflicts? ................................................................................. | **12b** | | |
| **c** Does the organization regularly and consistently monitor and enforce compliance with the policy? *If "Yes," describe in Schedule O how this is done* ................................................................ | **12c** | | |
| **13** Does the organization have a written whistleblower policy? ............................................. | **13** | | |
| **14** Does the organization have a written document retention and destruction policy? ..................... | **14** | | |
| **15** Did the process for determining compensation of the following persons include a review and approval by independent persons, comparability data, and contemporaneous substantiation of the deliberation and decision: | | | |
| **a** The organization's CEO, Executive Director, or top management official? ............................. | **15a** | | |
| **b** Other officers or key employees of the organization? ............................................... | **15b** | | |
| Describe the process in Schedule O. (see instructions) | | | |
| **16a** Did the organization invest in, contribute assets to, or participate in a joint venture or similar arrangement with a taxable entity during the year? ...................................................................... | **16a** | | |
| **b** If "Yes," has the organization adopted a written policy or procedure requiring the organization to evaluate its participation in joint venture arrangements under applicable federal tax law, and taken steps to safeguard the organization's exempt status with respect to such arrangements? .................................... | **16b** | | |

### Section C. Disclosure

**17** List the states with which a copy of this Form 990 is required to be filed

**18** Section 6104 requires an organization to make its Forms 1023 (or 1024 if applicable), 990, and 990-T (501(c)(3)s only) available for public inspection. Indicate how you make these available. Check all that apply.
☐ Own website　　☐ Another's website　　☐ Upon request

**19** Describe in Schedule O whether (and if so, how), the organization makes its governing documents, conflict of interest policy, and financial statements available to the public.

**20** State the name, physical address, and telephone number of the person who possesses the books and records of the organization:

146

| **Part VII** | Compensation of Officers, Directors, Trustees, Key Employees, Highest Compensated Employees, and Independent Contractors |

**Section A.** <u>Officers, Directors, Trustees, Key Employees, and Highest Compensated Employees</u>

**1a** Complete this table for all persons required to be listed. Use Schedule J-2 if additional space is needed.

    List all of the organization's **current** officers, directors, trustees (whether individuals or organizations), regardless of amount of compensation, and **current** key employees. Enter -0- in columns (D), (E), and (F) if no compensation was paid.

    List the organization's five **current** highest compensated employees (other than an officer, director, trustee, or key employee) who received reportable compensation (Box 5 of Form W-2 and/or Box 7 of Form 1099-MISC) of more than $100,000 from the organization and any related organizations.

    List all of the organization's **former** officers, key employees, and highest compensated employees who received more than $100,000 of reportable compensation from the organization and any related organizations.

    List all of the organization's **former directors or trustees** that received, in the capacity as a former director or trustee of the organization, more than $10,000 of reportable compensation from the organization and any related organizations.

List persons in the following order: individual trustees or directors; institutional trustees; officers; key employees; highest compensated employees; and former such persons.

☐ Check this box if the organization did not compensate any officer, director, trustee, or key employee.

| (A) Name and Title | (B) Average hours per week | (C) Position (check all that apply) | | | | | | (D) Reportable compensation from the organization (W-2/1099-MISC) | (E) Reportable compensation from related organizations (W-2/1099-MISC) | (F) Estimated amount of other compensation from the organization and related organizations |
|---|---|---|---|---|---|---|---|---|---|---|
| | | Individual trustee or director | Institutional trustee | Officer | Key employee | Highest compensated employee | Former | | | |
| | | | | | | | | | | |
| | | | | | | | | | | |
| | | | | | | | | | | |
| | | | | | | | | | | |
| | | | | | | | | | | |
| | | | | | | | | | | |
| | | | | | | | | | | |
| | | | | | | | | | | |
| | | | | | | | | | | |
| | | | | | | | | | | |
| | | | | | | | | | | |
| | | | | | | | | | | |
| | | | | | | | | | | |
| | | | | | | | | | | |
| | | | | | | | | | | |
| | | | | | | | | | | |
| | | | | | | | | | | |
| | | | | | | | | | | |

147

**Part VII** Section A. Officers, Directors, Trustees, Key Employees, and Highest Compensated Employees *(continued)*

| (A) Name and title | (B) Average hours per week | (C) Position (check all that apply) | | | | | | (D) Reportable compensation from the organization (W-2/1099-MISC) | (E) Reportable compensation from related organizations (W-2/1099-MISC) | (F) Estimated amount of other compensation from the organization and related organizations |
|---|---|---|---|---|---|---|---|---|---|---|
| | | Individual trustee or director | Institutional trustee | Officer | Key employee | Highest compensated employee | Former | | | |
| | | | | | | | | | | |
| | | | | | | | | | | |
| | | | | | | | | | | |
| | | | | | | | | | | |
| | | | | | | | | | | |
| | | | | | | | | | | |
| | | | | | | | | | | |
| | | | | | | | | | | |
| | | | | | | | | | | |
| | | | | | | | | | | |
| | | | | | | | | | | |
| | | | | | | | | | | |
| | | | | | | | | | | |
| | | | | | | | | | | |
| | | | | | | | | | | |
| | | | | | | | | | | |
| | | | | | | | | | | |
| | | | | | | | | | | |

**1b Total** ...........................................................................

**2** Total number of individuals (including those in 1a) who received more than $100,000 in reportable compensation from the organization

| | | Yes | No |
|---|---|---|---|
| **3** | Did the organization list any **former** officer, director or trustee, key employee, or highest compensated employee on line 1a? *If "Yes," complete Schedule J for such individual* ............................. **3** | | |
| **4** | For any individual listed on line 1a, is the sum of reportable compensation and other compensation from the organization and related organizations greater than $150,000? *If "Yes," complete Schedule J for such individual.* ................................................................................ **4** | | |
| **5** | Did any person listed on line 1a receive or accrue compensation from any unrelated organization for services rendered to the organization? *If "Yes," complete Schedule J for such person* ................ **5** | | |

**Section B. Independent Contractors**

**1** Complete this table for your five highest compensated independent contractors that received more than $100,000 of compensation from the organization.

| (A) Name and business address | (B) Description of services | (C) Compensation |
|---|---|---|
| | | |
| | | |
| | | |
| | | |
| | | |

**2** Total number of independent contractors (including those in 1) who received more than $100,000 in compensation from the organization

Form **990** (2008)

148

| Part VIII | Statement of Revenue | | | |
|---|---|---|---|---|
| | | **(A)** Total revenue | **(B)** Related or exempt function revenue | **(C)** Unrelated business revenue | **(D)** Revenue excluded from tax under sections 512, 513, or 514 |

**Contributions, gifts, grants and other similar amounts**

| | | | | | |
|---|---|---|---|---|---|
| **1a** Federated campaigns | 1a | | | | |
| **b** Membership dues | 1b | | | | |
| **c** Fundraising events | 1c | | | | |
| **d** Related organizations | 1d | | | | |
| **e** Government grants (contributions) | 1e | | | | |
| **f** All other contributions, gifts, grants, and similar amounts not included above | 1f | | | | |
| **g** Noncash contributions included in lines 1a-1f: $ | | | | | |
| **h** **Total.** Add lines 1a–1f | | | | | |

**Program Service Revenue**

| | | Business Code | | | |
|---|---|---|---|---|---|
| **2a** | | | | | |
| **b** | | | | | |
| **c** | | | | | |
| **d** | | | | | |
| **e** | | | | | |
| **f** All other program service revenue | | | | | |
| **g** **Total.** Add lines 2a–2f | | | | | |

**Other Revenue**

| | | | | | |
|---|---|---|---|---|---|
| **3** Investment income (including dividends, interest, and other similar amounts) | | | | | |
| **4** Income from investment of tax-exempt bond proceeds | | | | | |
| **5** Royalties | | | | | |

| | | (i) Real | (ii) Personal | | | |
|---|---|---|---|---|---|---|
| **6a** Gross Rents | | | | | | |
| **b** Less: rental expenses | | | | | | |
| **c** Rental income or (loss) | | | | | | |
| **d** Net rental income or (loss) | | | | | | |

| | | (i) Securities | (ii) Other | | | |
|---|---|---|---|---|---|---|
| **7a** Gross amount from sales of assets other than inventory | | | | | | |
| **b** Less: cost or other basis and sales expenses | | | | | | |
| **c** Gain or (loss) | | | | | | |
| **d** Net gain or (loss) | | | | | | |

| | | | | | |
|---|---|---|---|---|---|
| **8a** Gross income from fundraising events (not including $ of contributions reported on line 1c). See Part IV, line 18 | a | | | | |
| **b** Less: direct expenses | b | | | | |
| **c** Net income or (loss) from fundraising events | | | | | |
| **9a** Gross income from gaming activities. See Part IV, line 19 | a | | | | |
| **b** Less: direct expenses | b | | | | |
| **c** Net income or (loss) from gaming activities | | | | | |
| **10a** Gross sales of inventory, less returns and allowances | a | | | | |
| **b** Less: cost of goods sold | b | | | | |
| **c** Net income or (loss) from sales of inventory | | | | | |

| | Miscellaneous Revenue | Business Code | | | |
|---|---|---|---|---|---|
| **11a** | | | | | |
| **b** | | | | | |
| **c** | | | | | |
| **d** All other revenue | | | | | |
| **e** **Total.** Add lines 11a–11d | | | | | |
| **12** **Total Revenue.** Add lines 1h, 2g, 3, 4, 5, 6d, 7d, 8c, 9c, 10c, and 11e | | | | | |

| **Part IX** | **Statement of Functional Expenses** |

Section 501(c)(3) and 501(c)(4) organizations must complete all columns.
All other organizations must complete column (A) but are not required to complete columns (B), (C), and (D).

| *Do not include amounts reported on lines 6b, 7b, 8b, 9b, and 10b of Part VIII.* | **(A)** Total expenses | **(B)** Program service expenses | **(C)** Management and general expenses | **(D)** Fundraising expenses |
|---|---|---|---|---|
| **1** Grants and other assistance to governments and organizations in the U.S. See Part IV, line 21 | | | | |
| **2** Grants and other assistance to individuals in the U.S. See Part IV, line 22 ............. | | | | |
| **3** Grants and other assistance to governments, organizations, and individuals outside the U.S. See Part IV, lines 15 and 16 ....... | | | | |
| **4** Benefits paid to or for members .......... | | | | |
| **5** Compensation of current officers, directors, trustees, and key employees ............. | | | | |
| **6** Compensation not included above, to disqualified persons (as defined under section 4958(f)(1)) and persons described in section 4958(c)(3)(B) .... | | | | |
| **7** Other salaries and wages ................ | | | | |
| **8** Pension plan contributions (include section 401(k) and section 403(b) employer contributions) .... | | | | |
| **9** Other employee benefits ................ | | | | |
| **10** Payroll taxes ........................... | | | | |
| **11** Fees for services (non-employees): | | | | |
| **a** Management ........................... | | | | |
| **b** Legal ................................... | | | | |
| **c** Accounting .............................. | | | | |
| **d** Lobbying ............................... | | | | |
| **e** Professional fundraising services. See Part IV, line 17 | | | | |
| **f** Investment management fees ............. | | | | |
| **g** Other ................................... | | | | |
| **12** Advertising and promotion ............... | | | | |
| **13** Office expenses ........................ | | | | |
| **14** Information technology ................... | | | | |
| **15** Royalties .............................. | | | | |
| **16** Occupancy ............................. | | | | |
| **17** Travel ................................. | | | | |
| **18** Payments of travel or entertainment expenses for any federal, state, or local public officials | | | | |
| **19** Conferences, conventions, and meetings . | | | | |
| **20** Interest ................................ | | | | |
| **21** Payments to affiliates ................... | | | | |
| **22** Depreciation, depletion, and amortization . | | | | |
| **23** Insurance .............................. | | | | |
| **24** Other expenses. Itemize expenses not covered above. (Expenses grouped together and labeled miscellaneous may not exceed 5% of total expenses shown on line 25 below.) | | | | |
| **a** | | | | |
| **b** | | | | |
| **c** | | | | |
| **d** | | | | |
| **e** | | | | |
| **f** All other expenses | | | | |
| **25** **Total functional expenses.** Add lines 1 through 24f | | | | |
| **26** **Joint Costs.** Check here ☐ if following SOP 98-2. Complete this line only if the organization reported in column (B) joint costs from a combined educational campaign and fundraising solicitation .................... | | | | |

**Part X**   **Balance Sheet**

| | | | | (A)<br>Beginning of year | | | (B)<br>End of year |
|---|---|---|---|---|---|---|---|
| **Assets** | 1 | Cash—non-interest-bearing ................................... | | | 1 | | |
| | 2 | Savings and temporary cash investments ........................... | | | 2 | | |
| | 3 | Pledges and grants receivable, net ............................... | | | 3 | | |
| | 4 | Accounts receivable, net ....................................... | | | 4 | | |
| | 5 | Receivables from current and former officers, directors, trustees, key employees, or other related parties. Complete Part II of Schedule L . | | | 5 | | |
| | 6 | Receivables from other disqualified persons (as defined under section 4958(f)(1)) and persons described in section 4958(c)(3)(B). Complete Part II of Schedule L ............................................. | | | 6 | | |
| | 7 | Notes and loans receivable, net .................................. | | | 7 | | |
| | 8 | Inventories for sale or use ...................................... | | | 8 | | |
| | 9 | Prepaid expenses and deferred charges ........................... | | | 9 | | |
| | 10a | Land, buildings, and equipment: cost basis | 10a | | | | |
| | b | Less: accumulated depreciation. Complete Part VI of Schedule D .................. | 10b | | 10c | | |
| | 11 | Investments—publicly traded securities ........................... | | | 11 | | |
| | 12 | Investments—other securities. See Part IV, line 11 ................ | | | 12 | | |
| | 13 | Investments—program-related. See Part IV, line 11 ............... | | | 13 | | |
| | 14 | Intangible assets ............................................. | | | 14 | | |
| | 15 | Other assets. See Part IV, line 11 ............................... | | | 15 | | |
| | 16 | **Total assets.** Add lines 1 through 15 (must equal line 34) .......... | | | 16 | | |
| **Liabilities** | 17 | Accounts payable and accrued expenses ........................... | | | 17 | | |
| | 18 | Grants payable ............................................... | | | 18 | | |
| | 19 | Deferred revenue ............................................. | | | 19 | | |
| | 20 | Tax-exempt bond liabilities ..................................... | | | 20 | | |
| | 21 | Escrow account liability. Complete Part IV of Schedule D ......... | | | 21 | | |
| | 22 | Payables to current and former officers, directors, trustees, key employees, highest compensated employees, and disqualified persons. Complete Part II of Schedule L ........................... | | | 22 | | |
| | 23 | Secured mortgages and notes payable to unrelated third parties .... | | | 23 | | |
| | 24 | Unsecured notes and loans payable ............................... | | | 24 | | |
| | 25 | Other liabilities. Complete Part X of Schedule D ................... | | | 25 | | |
| | 26 | **Total liabilities.** Add lines 17 through 25 ...................... | | | 26 | | |
| **Net Assets or Fund Balances** | | **Organizations that follow SFAS 117, check here** ☐ **and complete lines 27 through 29, and lines 33 and 34.** | | | | | |
| | 27 | Unrestricted net assets ........................................ | | | 27 | | |
| | 28 | Temporarily restricted net assets ................................. | | | 28 | | |
| | 29 | Permanently restricted net assets ................................ | | | 29 | | |
| | | **Organizations that do not follow SFAS 117, check here** ☐ **and complete lines 30 through 34.** | | | | | |
| | 30 | Capital stock or trust principal, or current funds ................. | | | 30 | | |
| | 31 | Paid-in or capital surplus, or land, building, or equipment fund .... | | | 31 | | |
| | 32 | Retained earnings, endowment, accumulated income, or other funds | | | 32 | | |
| | 33 | Total net assets or fund balances ................................ | | | 33 | | |
| | 34 | Total liabilities and net assets/fund balances ..................... | | | 34 | | |

**Part XI**   **Financial Statements and Reporting**

| | | Yes | No |
|---|---|---|---|
| 1 | Accounting method used to prepare the Form 990: ☐ Cash  ☐ Accrual  ☐ Other | | |
| 2a | Were the organization's financial statements compiled or reviewed by an independent accountant? .... | 2a | |
| b | Were the organization's financial statements audited by an independent accountant? ................. | 2b | |
| c | If "Yes" to lines 2a or 2b, does the organization have a committee that assumes responsibility for oversight of the audit, review, or compilation of its financial statements and selection of an independent accountant? .... | 2c | |
| 3a | As a result of a federal award, was the organization required to undergo an audit or audits as set forth in the Single Audit Act and OMB Circular A-133? ......................................................... | 3a | |
| b | If "Yes," did the organization undergo the required audit or audits? ........................................ | 3b | |

151

## Contractors

All non-profits are required to comply with federal, state, and local laws and regulations. For instance, non-profits are required to file 1099s related to vendors, as any other business. Actually 990-Part V question 1a reads, "Enter the number reported in Box 3 of Form 1096, Annual Summary and Transmittal of U.S. Information Returns. Enter-0- if not applicable." (The 1096 is the transmittal form for 1099s.) The IRS has become aware that many organizations are not following the rules as they should and wants more non-profits to consider and to comply with the 1099/1096 filing requirement.

## Sales Tax

Non-profits may owe sales, excise, or use taxes on fundraising and other revenue-generating events, depending on the state.

This issue is important because it affects fundraising net revenues. Check with the state where the non-profit organization is located about local taxes and possible exemptions. Certain exemptions need to be filed and approved before fundraising events; otherwise the organization owes sales tax as per state.

For California non-profit issues, you can go to this link:
http://www.taxes.ca.gov/exemptbus.shtml

# Payroll

Payroll processes for non-profits are the same as for-profits. A GAO study presented in June 2007 noted that many non-profits were not complying with federal law, including those receiving federal funding:

"GAO found nearly 55,000 exempt organizations had almost $1 billion in unpaid taxes as of September 30, 2006. About 1,500 of these entities each had over $100,000 in federal tax debts with some owing tens of millions of dollars. The majority of this debt represented payroll taxes and associated penalties and interest dating as far back as the early 1980s. Willful failure to remit payroll taxes is a felony under U.S. tax law. The $1 billion figure is understated because some exempt organizations have understated tax liabilities or did not file tax returns." http://www.gao.gov/new.items/d07563.pdf

Payroll taxes and reporting compliance should be done both at federal and state/local levels. Making sure that all deductions are taken and all taxes are paid is important. Many times payroll processing firms are misinformed on the payroll responsibilities and process payroll with mistakes. Check with the state about specific state payroll considerations, including unemployment and disability insurance.

An interesting concept for non-profits is the issue of employees being required to work as volunteers. This can be sticky. If anybody is required to volunteer, then it is not really volunteering. Employees may be eligible for overtime pay and if the organization doesn't pay up, it may be in trouble with the government. I suggest NOT requiring employees to volunteer and if they do, then pay them, or, in the case of exempt employees, give them paid-time-off credits for the volunteering time.

The IRS and states mind if an employee is being treated as an independent contractor. The rules apply to both for-profit and non-profit organizations. The non-profit organization doesn't get any breaks because it receives government funds.

Per the IRS, the common law rules are:

1. Behavioral: Does the company control or have the right to control what the worker does and how the worker does his or her job?
2. Financial: Are the business aspects of the worker's job controlled by the payer? (These include things like how worker is paid, whether expenses are reimbursed, who provides tools/supplies, etc.)
3. Type of Relationship: Are there written contracts or employee type benefits (i.e. pension plan, insurance, vacation pay, etc.)? Will the relationship continue and is the work performed a key aspect of the business?

http://www.irs.gov/businesses/small/article/0,,id=99921,00.html

Depending on the answers to these questions, contractors may be re-classified as employees and the organization will owe lots of money in taxes, interest, and penalties.

Non-profits and taxes are not strangers. Even though non-profits' goal is not to have a profit, certain transactions can be taxed, depending on state law. Non-profits are not above the law when classifying employees and contractors and a mistake in this area can be very costly.

# CHAPTER 9

## *INTERNAL CONTROLS*

*"If men were angels, no government would be necessary. If angels were to govern men, neither external nor internal controls on government would be necessary."*

James Madison, fourth President of the U. S.

Concepts of internal controls are not new. Internal controls have been getting more attention lately because of the Enron scandal and its fallout, such as the Sarbanes and Oxley Act of 2002 (SOX). Internal controls focus on checks and balances, ethics, proper governance, responsibility, and accountability.

The Sarbanes and Oxley Act was directed toward public companies, but there are two provisions that are applicable to all corporations, including non-profits. These provisions are:

- Whistle-blower protection – SOX provides new protection for whistle-blowers, making it illegal for a corporation to retaliate against employees who report suspected illegal activities.
- Document destruction--Per SOX, it is illegal to destroy or alter any document to prevent its use in an official proceeding, such as bankruptcy.

You can read the Act at http://frwebgate.access.gpo.gov/

In addition to these specific provisions, many states enacted their own SOX compliance laws for non-profit organizations. For example, California passed a "Non-profit Integrity Act" requiring non-profits with budgets over $2 million to have an annual audit by an independent auditor and the results to be shared with the public and the Attorney General.

The government has become very interested in non-profit corporate governance and has specific questions about this issue in the newly designed tax return 990. Internal controls and governance are the on-going trend to watch. This can be seen as a higher standard for businesses to comply with to avoid errors and misappropriations.

It is just a matter of time before the full Sarbanes and Oxley Act is adapted to non-profits. Accountability is essential for any non-profit organization. As a matter of fact, some boards require compliance with SOX and some non-profits, especially large ones, are in compliance with many sections of the Act.

To comply with the new standards, an organization could set up an Independent Audit Committee. Members of this committee cannot be part of the management team and cannot be employees of the organization. The organization could also set up whistle-blower processes and written policies regarding document destruction.

The CEO/CFO could directly review and sign off on the non-profit's tax returns and final annual reports before they are submitted. The Board of Directors could review the taxes and annual reports. Actually, the 990 specifically requests information about how the 990 is reviewed before submission. The point is to make top management accountable.

A way to show management accountability is to develop written policies and procedures, showing that the organization meets the new standard for operations. Non-profits that comply voluntarily with SOX legislation may have a competitive advantage over others that are clueless. Complying and being aware of SOX can enhance the image of a non-profit by showing solid internal infrastructure. Funders appreciate internal controls these days. It even can be used in marketing/development as an edge in competing for dollars out there!

*Some questions showing up in the 990: Does the organization have a written whistle-blower policy? ... Does the organization have a written document retention and destruction policy?*

Some of the other SOX items that non-profits could implement include:

- Prohibiting loans to executives and board members
- Implementing a code of ethics policy
- Avoiding conflicts of interest, especially involving any business transactions
- Establishing audit independence by making sure the audit firm is not allowed to also perform consulting services

*Per 990, organizations should avoid conflicts of interest. 990-Section B. Policies 12a asks, "Does the organization have a written conflict of interest policy?" 12b asks, "Are officers, directors or trustees and key employees required to disclose annually interests that could give rise to conflicts?" 12c asks, "Does the organization regularly and consistently monitor and enforce compliance with policy? If 'Yes,' describe in Schedule O how this is done."*

Next, we will discuss ways to create and maintain good internal controls. It is not that tough. Many of the items are just common sense and many organizations already may have good controls and not be aware of this.

# Controls for Cash/Revenue

Cash is not simply money, but also checks and credit card payments. Clearly, hard cash is one of the riskiest assets and one that can be lost or stolen easily. A non-profit should have a safe (preferably bolted to a wall or floor) with the code known to limited personnel to safeguard cash, un-deposited checks and other valuables. Do not keep it in a desk or in another unsafe place.

Hard cash is usually a problem in times of appeal or other fundraising events. A strategy should be in place for cash to be put in a safe place ASAP. I have been to events where envelopes with pledges, checks, and cash were thrown away in the trash can by mistake. Have a group of people responsible for picking up cash, checks, and pledges and put them in a safe place promptly.

"Cash" also comes in the form of credit card receipts, which must be processed. Make sure to get donors' signatures on any purchase. Many times donors are drunk or distracted when buying auctioned items or when making donations and they charge-back later on. If an organization doesn't have a donor's signature, it loses the money in a challenge situation where the donor forgets about purchases or donations.

What do you do about telephone sales of tickets or donations? Ask for as much information as possible, including the CSV numbers on credit cards and zip codes.

Sometimes cash is also received in the mail, or people walk in with large amounts of cash. Many organizations have the policy of not accepting cash over a certain amount. Have "blurbs" in promotional materials discouraging the use of hard cash. This is the easiest asset to lose.

A website can be used for donations or payments for events or programs. It is a great way to decrease the risk of loss or misappropriation of funds. It can be a bit expensive, but nowadays, it is the way to go.

Many organizations use lockboxes in banks for daily processing or for special campaigns. The advantage of lockboxes is that the money goes to the bank right away and there is no internal processing by people. Lockboxes can process credit card slips/payments as well. This can be important on high volume situations. Usually lockbox staff sends organizations faxes or online copies of all paperwork received daily. This service doesn't come cheap with banks charging fees per check and credit card slips, but it may be worth it.

With the Internet becoming as popular as it is, lockboxes are losing their appeal. Many people are simply going to use the Internet, and there may not be volume significant to justify lockbox usage in the near future, but it can be an option. Contact the bank to see if lockboxes make sense. The bank also may have good deals for credit card transactions online via its website.

Standard basic cash controls are:

- ❖ Two people should count cash, not just one.
- ❖ Two people should open the mail.
- ❖ Cash and checks should be deposited the same day or next. Many banks offer free courier service for limited cash deposits.
- ❖ Cash and checks should be counted and put in a safe, not in a locked desk drawer.
- ❖ Receipts should be given on all cash transactions. Copies of receipts are kept.
- ❖ Organizations could prohibit the receipt of cash over a certain amount and accept only checks or credit cards for the transactions/donations. In a non-profit I know, the maximum cash amount allowed was $1,000. (Over $12,000 in cash disappeared before I was hired at one non-profit.)
- ❖ Organizations could bond employees handling cash.
- ❖ Organizations should hire people with clean credit and criminal records.
- ❖ Bank reconciliations should be done monthly, without delays and any discrepancies investigated.
- ❖ Bank statements could be forwarded first to someone who is not involved in accounting. This person could review deposits and check/copies of checks for amounts and signatures.
- ❖ Wire transfers should involve at least two pre-authorized people.
- ❖ Petty cash should be counted monthly and any expense should have a receipt explaining it. Surprise counts of petty cash are also advisable.

❖ People handling cash should rotate and take vacations to let someone else do the job. (Many times fraud and other problems are discovered when the person usually in this role is not present.)
❖ Regular surprise counts of cash should be part of internal controls. The counts should be matched to receipts or other documents.

Many times checks come into the organization without any flyer or papers. These checks could be just general donations, but could be for programs as well. Accounting personnel may spend lots of time calling the donors and requesting more information. To avoid this problem, the organization could have a "blurb" on all its program flyers asking people to indicate the specific program in check payments. This decreases the volume of "mystery" checks coming in.

## Receivables

In a non-profit organization, receivables are usually pledges receivable or grants receivable. Pledges receivable are risky because people or firms can change their minds and not fulfill the pledge commitment. Usually there is no recourse to collect. Membership receivable and other types of receivables where the donor receives benefits for the receivable are much more likely to be collected.

Besides receivables not being collectible, another risk is that people make payments, but they may get lost, misappropriated, or stolen. If an organization has good controls over cash, these issues may be avoided. A control would be for donors who complain about lost or misapplied payments to contact someone not involved with accounting.

A particular risk in the grant receivable area is about the grantor requiring certain compliance items to be performed and if not, the organization may need to return the funds, receive much less, or simply stop getting funds. I worked in a medical-related non-profit where the therapist working there didn't have all the educational and experience required for the position. The organization had a $100,000 reduction in its grant for the following year. It was material for the organization and it had to cut programs to absorb the cut.

Another risk of grants receivable is that the contract may close and not all expenses may be presented to be reimbursed on time. I have seen an organization not being attentive regarding grant contracts that have been closed. The organization received funds by mistake for years with nobody noticing it. Unfortunately, the non-profit had to return hundreds of thousands of dollars once the issue was discovered later by auditors. Not pretty. As suggested in another chapter, a summary on all contracts with dates and other information can avoid this type of problem. Don't count on grantors to promptly catch errors. They may catch it later, when funds have been used up. Many times auditors find the issues a year or so later.

Non-profits usually have an allowance for doubtful accounts based on historical collections. The writing off of delinquent accounts should be done by executive management in writing. No accounting personnel should be able to decide who is to be written off and not. I have seen situations where funds have been misplaced and accounts were written off by accounting with no backup documentation. This situation presents uncomfortable issues: about people being friends and bribes in lieu of discounts, etc. Make sure to avoid this problem by properly segregating the duties of who is approving the discounts from who is booking them. Also, keep it all in writing.

Some receivables/revenues are to be used in a certain program and are restricted. The organization should book the receivables/revenues where they belong. If someone donated $10 or $10,000 for a certain program, say a construction project, the accounting for these funds should reflect that. Some organizations have policies to book in restricted funds donations over a certain amount, say $500. Anything less than that is booked in the general fund area. If this is the case, this policy should be disclosed in marketing and other publications requesting the funds.

Another area of potential problems involves accounts receivable and revenues by credit card written in forms. Credit cards can be charged multiple times: Forms can be faxed and the credit card charged; forms can then be mailed and credit cards are charged again. Or the fax is copied, given to accounting and the credit card is charged again. What can be done to minimize this common problem?

-Use the website instead of paper forms whenever possible

-The accounting department should process only originals, not copies of forms

-The fax machine should have a color marker to identify faxes as original faxes

-Forms with instructions to fax payments should indicate that faxing and sending originals are not necessary; do one OR the other, but not both

Accounts receivable aging reports should be compared and reconciled with the general ledger at least once a month, even in integrated systems. Many times journal entries may have been made in the general ledger and not reversed by mistake.

Make sure to keep a good filing system, such as using last names of donors. This is especially important for temporarily restricted funds, when donors give for a specific purpose. Not only is it helpful to identify the donor, but also as back up to the restricted fund(s). Organizations could have many restricted funds, one for each program or by type of restriction, such as "Building Fund" for maintenance of the current building, or "Educational Books" for purchases of books.

Many large businesses match contributions made by employees and keeping both employee and business "linked" is a must online or on paper.

Other common receivables controls are:

❖ The people receiving money or opening the mail should not be the same ones who handle accounts receivable.

❖ Analysis of accounts receivable, an aging report, can be reviewed by management to identify unusual transactions and possible delinquencies.

❖ Any credits/decreases in receivables should be approved by management not involved in accounts receivable. (I have seen employees giving fake credits to people who they had a relationship with.)

❖ All receivables must have written backup confirming the receivable as valid and existent.

❖ Appropriate controls should exist on computerized systems to assure the privacy of donors, especially for those who request anonymity.

❖ People running accounts receivable should be required to take vacations. (Many times fraud and other problems are discovered when the person is not present.)

## Accounts Payable-Expenses

Accounts payable is part of any business, including non-profits. Bills need to be paid and accounting staff needs to know whether the expense is related to the general fund or to any program or grant. Many grants require periodic expense reporting, making expense identification a must.

Be aware of scam artists focusing on non-profits. I witnessed a scam in a non-profit organization involving printer cartridges. The scam was to send out bad cartridges and then send a bill for payment. Nobody really ordered the cartridges, but the scammer had a name of someone in administration who supposedly ordered the items. When asked, the person couldn't remember ordering anything. It was a scam that worked for at least one year. It stopped because the scammer used the name of someone no longer with the organization who couldn't have ordered anything. Plus, there was a new person in charge of technology, so the scam stopped.

Office supply fraud is well-known to the Federal Trade Commission, including the targeting of small businesses and non-profits. "The Imaging Supplies Coalition," an organization that combats telemarketing fraud and other illegal activities that affect its members and their customers, estimates that office supply fraud costs small businesses and non-profit organizations an estimated $200 million a year. www.ftc.gov

Visit the http://www.FTC.gov frequently and look out for known scams.

Just because an organization receives a bill, that doesn't mean that it should be paid fast, without questions. Accounting needs to confirm, in writing, that items were received in good condition and/or that services were rendered. Accounting should get packing slips acknowledging receipt of goods that are matched with invoices. If items are returned, the accounting department should also be notified for possible credit or refund.

Many organizations use a purchase order system with department heads pre-approving expenses. This is a good system to maintain control over purchases before they happen. It is also a good information source for accounting department staff, who more often than not, receive bills without knowing what they were for or who placed the order. A lot of time is wasted by accounts payable staff, trying to figure out what bills are for; so people allowed to make purchases should tell vendors to put more information about the purchase in invoices for faster payment, and should use a purchase order if applicable.

A purchase order system is advisable, especially for large purchases. A P.O. can be filled out and can be compared to the budget BEFORE a purchase is made. This system helps keep expenses in line with the budget and provides good control. Most expenses could run through P.O.s. Many accounting systems allow non-accounting personnel to create and approve purchases, including inserting accounting codes. Often, the accounting codes are not be correct. A P.O. could be set up using a grant number that expired before it was fully used. In this case, the accounting code is correct, but not the grant coding.

A common problem for accounts payable is double paying of vendors. Accounting software these days has a feature to reject duplicate invoices and that is a great control. Organizations should also have policies not to pay on statements-only invoices. Statements should be kept for any credit memos. Many times vendors have credits for the organization, but don't apply them to any specific invoice. Credit memos could be used to identify credits and use them in current invoices.

Producing a clean vendor master listing is challenging, but worth the effort. If not, the same vendor shows up more than once, making vendor history and aging reports distorted. I suggest conducting a vendor cleanup at least once a year. Make sure Social Security numbers/Federal IDs and other personal information on contractors is in the system and is kept safe with only authorized personnel having access to it.

Accounts payable should be reconciled to the general ledger monthly to identify errors and omissions. Sometimes journal entries may need to be reversed or not all transactions need to flow through general ledger. Credits should be applied to any open invoices; I have seen credits "hidden" in the system for years.

---

*Creating fictitious vendors and paying them is a well-known fraud. To avoid this problem, someone not directly related to Accounts Payable processing should review vendor reports, especially change reports and new vendor reports. Sometimes it is easier to put the reports in a worksheet and sort by name and/or last invoice payment dates.*

As with the for-profit firms, 1099s are distributed to vendors and filed with the government with 1096 forms, as per federal law. Local and state laws regarding contractors are to be followed. Non-profits don't get breaks in this area. Sorry.

Many times, Accounts Payable needs to reimburse employees for expenses. Reimbursement requests must be approved by a supervisor and must contain receipts and other backup to justify the reimbursement.

Advances to employees are to be avoided. Once advances are given, then employees need to return unused funds and present receipts to justify expenses. This is a very risky process because employees may lose funds; they may use them for personal items, or may not have all of the receipts.

Corporate credit cards, when used properly, replace the need for any advances. Corporate credit cards are to be used by only a couple of people and only for business expenses. Contact the bank for corporate cards' availability. I have seen corporate cards getting out of control with people charging for personal items. Once that starts happening, it is time to remind users of proper use and pull them off the account if necessary.

Checks used to pay for expenses are to be signed by managers not involved in the accounting process. It is a good control to require two signatures on checks over a certain amount, say $1,000. Many banks offer check safety services where only checks on daily lists are paid by the bank. This prevents fraud and has become popular, especially with large non-profits.

Voided checks are kept in a file for at least one year. They are taken out of the outstanding check list during bank reconciliation.  Be careful with this issue--many systems are set up to void checks as of the day of the check, not as of today. This can create a nightmare. Make sure the voided checks are done as of today and not in the past.

Also note that in many accounting systems, when a check is voided today it will not show up in a re-print of past outstanding checks. So, it is a good idea to print out outstanding check lists and keep them with the bank reconciliation because the same list may be different if reprinted.

Escheating old checks to the state is a common process. Usually, when uncashed checks are older than a year, they "go" to the state. So, it is important to keep outstanding checks up-to-date.  Don't be in a hurry to send them to the state because often un-cashed checks are not "real"--they are voided checks not voided in the system.  Confirm with vendors before escheating the checks.

To avoid double-paying bills, accounting staff normally stamps each invoice "PAID" as payments are processed. In many accounting departments, the account used is written up in the invoice. A copy of the check or the voucher can be attached to the paid invoice for a full packet.

The person doing accounts receivables or payables should not be the one performing bank reconciliations, if at all possible, due to proper segregation of duties. If not possible, then a manager or someone within the department should review and sign off on the bank reconciliations monthly.

## Payroll

Some organizations operate based only on volunteers, but many need employees and it is common for payroll to be the biggest expense in the financial statements. Many organizations use outside payroll services, but some prefer to run payroll in-house. Payroll can be complicated. In many organizations, especially when funded by government grants, everyone files time sheets--even the President--to justify charging grants real time and not estimated time. Nowadays many organizations are using electronic time-keeping devices and electronic time sheets. This cuts down on time and confusion.

In paper or in electronic format, time sheets must be approved by supervisors to make sure hours and overtime were authorized. Each employee also should have paperwork filled out with Human Resources and should visit the HR department personally. I know a non-profit where a program supervisor made up an employee with a fake Social Security number and payroll paperwork. The "employee" was paid for about six months and the supervisor cashed the paychecks. It was only after there was a problem with the time sheet of this person (all fake) that the Human Resources manager got involved and the fraud was discovered. The point of the story: Human Resources must be involved when hiring any new employees and must personally meet all new employees.

To make sure that payroll records are correct, department managers/directors can review and sign off on payroll registers regarding their department at least once a quarter. Many department heads get the dollar amount of their departments' payroll expenses through internal regular reporting, but not the details. So, having them look at who is working in each department, who has received sick days, vacations, etc. is very helpful in keeping payroll correct.

If a paycheck is not cashed within a week, an employee needs to be contacted. Sometimes he/she lost the check or forgot about it. It happens. One issue I have seen often with payroll is about terminated people still getting paid because payroll didn't know about the termination. It is important for Human Resources and managers to notify the payroll department when people quit or are let go. Final checks need to be cut and the payroll system needs to be updated as well.

As a control, a manager, controller, or treasurer should look at payroll registers and change reports to make sure the person running payroll is not paying himself/herself unauthorized overtime or salary increases--a common fraud.

More than one person should know how to run payroll. This is a critical part of business that cannot be late; people need to be paid on time. So, if something happens to the person doing payroll, what is the plan? This is not just for payroll time, but also for terminations, when a check needs to be cut and signed the same day. Have more than one person know how to run payroll and cut checks.

Having a personnel manual is important. The manual should contain information about types of employees, paid holidays, vacation policies, etc. Any changes to the manual should be approved by an executive or board of directors.

All payroll-related documents, including time sheets, should be kept in a safe, locked place. Only authorized personnel should be allowed to see reports containing Social Security numbers and other information. Be very careful working with temporary workers in this area.

## Equipment

Equipment could be purchased or donated to the non-profit and, depending of value, equipment could be capitalized. Equipment, such as computers, should be inventoried and marked. A list of equipment is to be updated for obsolescence, theft, or exchanges. This is especially important for large organizations with offices in multiple locations.

It is easy for laptop computers to disappear, and special software can be installed on the laptops to identify their location via satellite. Make sure to conduct an equipment count and audit at least once a year and have it all tagged. Insurance policies usually require the annual review of asset listing, including equipment, anyway.

If equipment is purchased with government funds, there may be specific requirements about its maintenance and care. Proceeds from the sale or disposition of equipment purchased with government funding should be returned to the grantor or applied as a credit.

Computers and servers, usually expensive items, should be safeguarded against tampering and viruses. Appropriate software must be purchased, and access from outside the office should be restricted to only a few authorized employees. Purchasing protective software and providing a safe physical place for the computers/servers may be costly, but it comes with the territory.

Purchases and retirement/sales of equipment should be approved by management. Dispositions of old computers should be done very carefully, since they may have confidential information on them. Files can be recovered from formatted hard-drives, unless specific precautions are taken.

# Audit Standard Affecting Internal Controls

In 2006 a new auditing standard was promulgated, affecting non-profits. It was the SAS No. 112- *Communicating Internal Control Related Matters Identified in an Audit.* The main points of the standard were:

- Auditors cannot be part of a client's internal control. Being part of a client's internal control impairs auditors' independence. Audit cannot be a risk control for clients.

- The appointment of an individual who possesses a suitable skill set or, knowledge, and/or experience to review a service performed by the CPA firm is not a control. Having such an appointed person doesn't mean much as far as controls are concerned.

- SAS No. 112 doesn't call for the auditor to look for control deficiencies, but rather to evaluate them if they have been identified.

- A system of internal control over financial reporting does not end at the general ledger; it also includes controls over the preparation of the financial statements.

- To properly apply SAS No. 112 the auditor has to have a working knowledge of the COSO framework. COSO's *Internal Control-Integrated Framework* describes the elements of internal control over financial reporting. SAS No. 112 directs the auditor to evaluate control deficiencies when identified, and communicate certain deficiencies to management and those charged with governance.

(http://www.aicpa.org/download/practmon/sas_112_guidance.pdf)

SAS 112 covers classifying deficiencies as significant, material or not. The deficiencies relate to potential errors, not real errors and there are a lot of judgment calls in this area. That being said, there are also opportunities for negotiations with auditors.

The way auditors have been planning audits has been changed on many levels. Talk to the auditing firm and get an idea about what the CPA firm will do and will not do for the organization. CPAs may require organizations to generate their own GAAP-correct financial statements, disclosures, and other items not previously requested.

Internal controls must be an integral part of any business and non-profits are no exception. Auditors look for good controls that can prevent problems early on or that can identify issues after the fact. Many times internal controls are not perceived as being the fastest or most efficient way to conduct business. Why not have one or two people do it all? Why not let the accounts receivable person receive money, since he/she knows how to apply it? Because that opens the doors for misappropriations and mistakes.

Checks and balances in business processes are important and internal controls, applied properly, usually fit the bill.

# CHAPTER 10

## *SPECIAL CONSIDERATIONS*

*"Every business and every product has risks. You can't get around it."*

Lee Iacocca

In this chapter, we will cover some specific non-profit issues, usually not found in the for-profit world, including specific risks, budget, pension fund issues, HR issues, and technology usage. A summary about non-profit resources available online is presented as well.

### Risks

Once an organization receives the 501(c) 3 tax-exempt status, it needs to maintain it. Organizations can risk tax-exempt status if they engage in certain transactions, such as:

- Private benefit/inurement: This is about private benefit versus public benefit. The exempt organization should serve the public, not a private individual. Examples are excessive salaries or transfers of property to insiders at less than fair market value.

- Lobbying: This is about affecting legislation and if it is substantial, it can affect the 501 (c) 3 status of the organization.

- Political campaign activity: Organizations are not to engage in any political campaign activity, not to donate or to be involved in it.

- Activities generating excessive unrelated business income: Donations and other funds received by a non-profit are exempt from federal taxes, but there are certain activities that are not part of the organization mission and are taxed. Examples include sales commissions and membership list sales. When these become excessive, the actual exemption may be revoked.
www.irs.gov

Other risks affecting non-profits are related to the nature of the exempt organization. Like for-profits, non-profits have accounts receivable; however, unlike for-profits, the receivables may not be related to sales or services provided. Instead, they may be pledges receivable and grants receivable. Many times pledges cannot be collected and there is no legal recourse. Sometimes there is legal recourse, but it may not be good for the organization's image. Pledges receivable are not as safe as regular accounts receivable, especially in the case of long-term pledges. The risk for default is high and there is not much the organization can do to collect.

Another risk is with grant contracts is that they are not stable. They can change, especially with government grants, and the organization has no control over it. Governments may be facing a difficult budget period and funds may be cut across the board. Revenue stream may be unstable and the organization may need to plan for worst case scenarios- what programs to cut, who to lay off, etc.

A non-profit risk that usually non-profits have no control over is the change in legislation and the possibility of certain donations not being tax-deductible anymore. The government has been looking for ways to create more revenues at the federal and state level and it is possible for laws to change regarding donations. Congress has been looking into non-profits that seem to be too rich, appearing to be more like regular businesses rather than charities. The Senate Finance Committee is likely to hold hearings about charitable deductions in 2009 and beyond.

A particular issue for non-profits, especially newly created ones, is related to the founders of the organization. Many times the organization may grow and founders may not have the expertise to take the non-profit to the next level. Ideas that founders had may not apply anymore to where the organization is. It can be very hard for founders to let go of the organization. This problem also happens with small for-profit businesses that are growing, especially family-owned businesses.

Organizations should have transition plans to replace "baby boomer" staff and executives, who may have stayed in the job for decades and will be retiring soon. The new generation has different views and expectations of the workplace and finding an appropriate Executive Director may be tougher than anticipated.

Many organizations plan for disaster, earthquakes, and hurricanes, but what if the Executive Director leaves or becomes ill and cannot work? What is the plan? Many Executive Directors are tied in to major funders and if they are no longer working at the organization, it can be disastrous.

Make sure the organization has a plan with funders and all stakeholders aware of it. There's no need to be alarmist about this--just start talking about this subject. It is real and important.

## Budget

It is crucial for a non-profit to have an annual budget. It is the map to keep the organization in line with its goals and to keep expenses on check. Purchase order amounts are checked against budget numbers. Reports are created to compare actual numbers versus the budget and how much of the budget has been used up. Without a budget, an organization would be swimming in the dark with nothing to indicate if things are going according to plan or not. Budget and planning go together. The budget is also helpful in identifying errors in accounting. If there is a variance in a line item budget, maybe it is because of a mistake.

Budgets could be set up on a yearly basis and monthly. They could be created based on history and what is known at the time of the budget, so it doesn't make sense to create a budget too early in the game. I have seen organizations creating budgets for board approval six months early and that didn't work well. Too many programs and other things happened within the last six months and the budget had to be totally redone a month before the new fiscal year. Usually a budget created within the last two to three months of a prior year is better and more realistic.

Budgets are static throughout the year; however, many times, a "forecasted" amount can be used. This column in reports can be used as a tool to calculate the following year's budget numbers.

Budgets could be done on accrual basis or cash. Some organizations do both budgets to plan for cash shortages during the year.

The challenge with budgets is to make sure all expenses are covered by funding sources. The other side of this challenge is to make sure that no expense is funded by two or more sources. This can be difficult to maintain, especially if people move around. Instead of working 50 percent in a certain program, a person is working now only 10 percent in that program. What/who is funding the 40 percent difference? Decisions like this are very important to a non-profit organization.

Besides the regular non-profit budget, many organizations also have grant or project budgets that work in parallel. Usually the accounting budget is uploaded into the accounting system and the grant/project budget is uploaded into the grant/project module.

## Pension Plan

Similarly to for-profits, non-profits can set up a pension plan for employees, where employees can contribute a portion of their salary to a pension plan. In the non-profit world, this type of retirement plan is known as 403(b).

Contributions to a plan 403(b) are not taxable and there are requirements about eligibility, maximum limits on contributions, etc. You can read the entire code at http://www.irs.gov

Lately there have been changes to the administration of 403(b) plans, that went into effect January 1, 2009. This has been the first major change in over forty years.

Some of the changes are:

- Written plan formal documentation is required on all retirement plans.
- As employers' control and responsibility increase, terms required to administer the plan should be dictated appropriately.
- Employers are responsible for "meaningful notice." All employees should be given an "effective opportunity" to make or change an elective deferral.
- All employees are permitted to make contributions, except for the ones specifically excluded.
- Centralized recordkeeping is critical to proper compliance.
- Form 5500 needs to be filed.

401(k) plans can be used by non-profits as well as 401 (b).


## Human Resources Issues

"The workforce of the charitable non-profit sector represents 10.5% of the country's total workforce." (L.A. Times 8/24/08)

Hiring and keeping good employees is a challenge faced by non-profits. Many cannot compete for the best based on salary amounts. Nowadays, many cannot compete for the best on health benefits either. So, what is left? How can an organization attract and keep good employees?

Some ideas:

- Generous time-off policy
- Flexible working hours
- Possibility of employees working from home
- Assistance with transportation
- Opportunities for professional development
- Lots of heartfelt praise

Did you know that if you worked for the government or certain non-profits, your student loan may be forgiven? Non-profit employees will be eligible for loan forgiveness after making 120 monthly payments after October 1, 2007, while employed by non-profits or in other public sector jobs.

## Technology

Non-profits have the challenge of being technologically up-to-date and of securing donors' data. Many donors do not want to be recognized and many do not want to be bothered by people asking for money. So, a non-profit should have software to accommodate most of donors' wishes.

Database files should be backed up and kept outside the premises. This is not just accounting information, but also names, addresses, and information on donors. Every employee should sign a confidentiality agreement regarding donors. Nowadays it is easy to make backups and steal files, so make sure that the donor database is secure.

An interesting situation occurs when an organization has many chapters (branches) and they share one database. Some donors may not want to have their private information available to hundreds of people. If a donor is a celebrity, this issue is even more delicate. Be aware of this problem.

> *Ethical questions regarding donor databases to consider: Can the information be sold to another organization? Can it be shared? What if an organization tries to buy another one's database?*

Technology can be used by non-profits for fundraising, but organizations need to be smart about it. Make the organization's own website donor friendly. Make it easy, safe, and pleasant to donate through the website. As the website is being built, review back-office operations. If donors can make donations to several programs, then the software "behind the scenes" should be mapped to correct accounting codes/accounts. Many times the accounting software can interface directly with the website.

Technology can also backfire.  People don't appreciate getting floods of emails asking for donations. They also may not appreciate getting text-messages on their cell phones. If the organization is considering either using email or texting to fund-raise, make sure they know of possible bad consequences of these strategies.  Carefully planned and targeted, they can work pretty well, but otherwise....


## Resources

Organizations' websites that may help non-profit management in its daily activities:

Journal of Philanthropy: http://philanthropy.com/

Idealist: http://www.idealist.org/

American Society of Association Executives: http://www.asaecenter.org/

California Association of Non-Profits: http://www.canon-profits.org/

National Council of Non-profit Association: http://www.ncna.org/

AICPA www.aicpa.org offers conferences, tool kits for boards, etc.

The Non-Profit  Resource Center: http://www.nprcenter.org/

Non-profit resources for accountants:
http://www.1800net.com/nprc/index.html

Non-profits and use of technology:
http://www.nten.org/research/techimpact/research/bibliography

# **CONCLUSION**

On a final note, dealing with non-profits can be a challenge, but can be very rewarding as well. The non-profit sector badly needs qualified people--people with not only good intentions and hearts, but good technical skills: good finance people, qualified accountants, and treasurers.

I hope this book gives you a general roadmap to the non-profit's areas, issues, and peculiarities. The similarities to the for-profit sector are many, but the twists can confuse many professionals, even those with many years of overall experience.

Many times, the problem is vocabulary. For example, knowing what "temporarily restricted funds" really means can facilitate understanding and can set up the basis for meaningful discussions.

I trust that this book is able to help the overwhelmed accounting/finance professional to understand the industry with an overall view of its usual operations and issues. I wish I had something like this when I started working in the non-profit sector.

Best of luck in dealing with the challenges of the non-profit world!!

# ABOUT SHEILA SHANKER

Sheila G. Shanker is a CPA and MBA based in Culver City in sunny Southern California. Sheila's long experience in the non-profit sector has given her the inside track of what non-profits are really like and what the finance professional must know.

A prolific writer, Sheila has contributed to national magazines, such as *"Journal of Accountancy," "Architecture Business and Economics," "Teachers of Vision," and "Laundry Today."*

Sheila has written accounting courses, including online CPE courses about non-profit organizations. These courses are being offered by many online providers, such as www.cpedepot, www.cpethink.com, www.jncpe.com, etc.

As a consultant, Sheila has helped many organizations in their finance, accounting, and MIS issues. She works as a CFO–Controller-consultant with proven expertise in internal controls, re-organization of accounting/finance departments, hiring, training, improving workflow processes, and overall leadership in the finance area. She tackles problem areas with diplomacy and tact.

You can visit Sheila G. Shanker's website at www.webshanker.com, where you can contact her and learn more about her background and experience. You can also contact her directly at Sheila@webshanker.com

Made in the USA
Charleston, SC
29 January 2010